Family Finances And Beyond

Currency Of Courage

RATHANDEEP U

BlueRose ONE.com
Stories Matter
NewDelhi • London

BLUEROSE PUBLISHERS
India | U.K.

BlueRose ONE.com
Stories Matter
NewDelhi • London

For permissions requests or inquiries regarding this publication, please contact:

BLUEROSE PUBLISHERS
www.BlueRoseONE.com
info@bluerosepublishers.com
+91 8882 898 898
+4407342408967

ISBN: 978-93-7542-936-4

Cover design: Anuj
Typesetting: Tanya Raj Upadhyay

First Edition: May 2026

AUTHOR'S NOTE

Some stories have life and some life become stories. These small stories are based on instances of real people whom I have come across in life. Each one inspired me to move ahead in my life. In spite of many unfavourable incidents in their lives, they had the courage to step into a new uncomfortable zone of financial management, transitioned and became a better version of themselves, for themselves, and for their families. It's more inside than outside that makes us who we are.

The world of investing, budgeting, and wealth-building seems like a zone of no knowledge or looks like it's designed for someone else, someone with more experience, more privilege, or simply more confidence. As a woman, we often doubt whether conversations about money are considered comfortable, especially in an Indian context where the decisions are not in our control.

But over time, I learnt that financial freedom isn't about having all the answers; it's about asking the right questions and taking decisions and making consistent, empowered steps. Taking decisions that can change the course of your life. This book is my way of paying forward the lessons that changed my life, in the hope that they can do the same for you.

Whether you're just starting out, rebuilding after a setback, or looking to grow your wealth strategically, this book is for you. My goal is not just to share knowledge but to help you build unshakable confidence in taking bold decisions and managing your finances.

You deserve security, freedom, and peace of mind. Let's begin.

DEDICATION

I Dedicate This Book To

My mother,

Who taught me that faith and resilience aren't just words, they're a way of life. Every morning, she would remind us that "everything will work out, just have faith and keep moving forward." Her unwavering belief became the foundation upon which I built my own strength.

She was my first teacher in the art of delayed gratification. While other families rushed to buy the latest trends, she showed us the quiet power of waiting, saving, and choosing wisely. "The difference between us and others," she would say, "isn't what we earn, it's what we keep and how we grow it."

My mother had an eye for quality over quantity. She would choose one beautiful piece over ten mediocre ones, care for it lovingly, and use it until it had given its fullest service. She taught me that true luxury isn't about brands or status, it's about making thoughtful choices that honour both your money and your values.

Her genius lay in how she handled our requests for money. She never said no, but she created a system that made us partners in our own financial education. Those monthly pocket money submissions weren't just paperwork, they were gentle lessons in accountability. When we came to her with our spending details, she didn't judge; she simply helped us see where our money went and asked us if those choices aligned with our dreams.

She created a home where wishes weren't denied but were honoured at the right time. This wasn't deprivation, it was wisdom. She showed us that the sweetest victories come to those who wait, plan, and persist.

The pages of this book are filled with her nuggets of wisdom, now shared with you. For every woman who dreams of financial independence, may you find in these words the same strength, faith, and practical wisdom that my mother gave me.

To the woman who showed me that financial freedom isn't just about money, it's about creating a life where your values and your choices are in perfect harmony.

With endless gratitude and love.

ACKNOWLEDGEMENTS

To my mother, my first money mentor and life's greatest teacher. Your unwavering faith, frugal wisdom, and quiet strength are woven into every chapter of this book. You showed me that financial freedom isn't about how much we earn, but how wisely we steward our blessings.

To my father, for your resilience and the sacrifices that built the foundation of our family's stability. You said, "If you want to better your life, you do something about it, go to office from tomorrow "

To my mother-in-law & Father-in-law, for your unconditional support and for reminding me that a woman's financial independence is her greatest security.

To Umesh & Chavi, my spouse & my daughter, my rock, my sounding board, and my partners in every dream. Your strength gives me courage, and your belief in me outshines every doubt.

To my Guru Mahatria, for lighting the path with your grace and blessings. Your guidance to increase my area of influence has been a big motivation for this book.

To my family, near and far, for cheering me on through writing sessions and celebrating every milestone as your own.

To the incredible women who trusted me with their money stories, your struggles and triumphs are the heartbeat of this book.

To my publishing team, for refining my words and amplifying this message. Thank you for seeing the power in women's financial liberation.

Finally, to you, dear reader: May this book meet you exactly where you are, and remind you that your independence is not just possible, but inevitable.

GENERAL DISCLAIMER:

"The information in this book is for educational purposes only and should not be considered personalized financial advice. All investment decisions should be made based on your individual financial situation, risk tolerance, and goals. Please consult with a qualified financial advisor before making investment decisions."

Investment Risk Warning: *"All investments carry risk, including potential loss of principal. Past performance does not guarantee future results. The value of investments can go up or down, and you may receive back less than you invested."*

Regulatory Compliance: *"This book does not constitute an offer to sell or solicitation to buy any securities. The author is not a registered investment advisor or financial planner. Always verify current regulations and tax implications with appropriate professionals."*

Story Disclaimers: *"The stories in this book are based on real experiences or instances but names, details, and circumstances have been changed to protect privacy. Individual results may vary significantly."*

Market Specific: *"All financial products, regulations, and tax implications mentioned are based on Indian market conditions at the time of publication. Rules and regulations may change. Please verify current information with SEBI-registered advisors."*

Limitation of Liability: *"The author and publisher assume no responsibility for errors, omissions, or damages arising from the use of this information. Readers are responsible for their own financial decisions."*

Professional Advice Recommendation: *"This book is not a substitute for professional financial, tax, or legal advice. Please consult qualified professionals for guidance specific to your situation."*

ABOUT THE AUTHOR

Rathandeep Umesh is the founder and CEO of Consulting and Beyond, a Certified Business Valuer with an MBA in Finance and over 15 years of experience consulting businesses. Her journey to writing *Currency of Courage* began in the settings of her "Fun with Finance" workshops.

Having personally experienced the transformation from sizable debt to financial freedom, Rathandeep understood that financial independence wasn't just about numbers, it was about courage. Through her workshops, Rathandeep discovered something profound: it wasn't skill or knowledge that made the difference in women's financial lives, it was their ability to make brave decisions. She watched as women absorbed financial concepts, left inspired, but struggled to take those crucial first steps at home.

"I realized that these women had everything they needed in their subconscious," Rathandeep reflects. "They could see a better future for themselves, but something was holding them back from immediate action. That's when I knew I had to write this book."

Despite facing societal norms that discouraged women from pursuing financial independence, she worked alongside her spouse to pay off debt and achieve financial stability.

Her mission became clear: to help women achieve financial freedom and pursue their passions without being tethered to their jobs for money. Based in Chennai, she continues to consult organizations on cash flows and financial strategy while dedicating her passion to empowering women through financial literacy.

Currency of Courage is her love letter to all the women who attended her workshops, and to every woman who can envision a better financial future but needs that gentle push to begin. This book bridges the gap between knowing and doing, between dreaming and achieving.

TABLE OF CONTENTS

IN THE GARDEN

The wind caught a whiff of the fresh aroma of mini samosas stuffed with the sweetness of corn, tangy cheese, and a tinge of spinach. The six women sat in a peaceful garden by a serene lake. All six chairs aligned in a circle with trees around them. Their gatherings in the garden became a tradition over the months.

“Today marks the second anniversary of our usual getting together evening happiness.” Sita said

“Isn’t it strange and exciting at the same time when we look back and wonder how we all met at Meetha’s yearly food hall exhibitions.” Said Bhavani

“I never thought we’d meet up like this every month and it’s already been two years. I hope we continue our little tradition.” Shivani smiled at all her friends.

Bhavani opened a hot flask of tea and served it to everyone. Each one got their own cup as part of their promise to meet up every month. Geetha, Damini, and Meetha raised their cups and so did everyone else. Geetha raised a toast, "To many more of these warm and wonderful evenings."

"To warm and wonderful evenings." the women cheered.

The Spring breeze blew across the vast garden of shrubs and trees. All the ladies sat reminiscing about the times that went by and how they all met. It was like opening a box of chocolates with an appetising visual of a variety of lives and the stories that presented themselves in different flavours.

"Tell us, Sita." Bhavani asked, "You've been an inspiration to all of us. You've never worked in your life. Even then you were able to grow your family wealth despite all limitations. You've given us a bit of your life story but we want to know more. Don't hold back today."

"Oh you want me to start from the beginning?"

"Yes," Bhavani said, "And we want all the details. Don't leave anything out."

"Okay then, brace yourselves because my journey started when I stepped out of the kitchen."

"What do you mean?" Damini asked.

"So, here's how it all began..."

FROM THE KITCHEN TABLE TO A DREAM COME TRUE

PART 1

“Ma, where’s your breakfast?” Mohit asked.

Sita paused for a second without making eye contact with her son.

“Beta, your uncle has spoken to your father and me.” She looks at Amit, her husband sitting and focusing on his breakfast at the kitchen table. Noticing how he wanted her to go on, she continued to talk to Mohit, “He was asking if you would like to work at his shop…”

She didn’t know what else to say after ‘shop’. Allowing her pause to beckon her son’s ability to connect the dots, hoping he could process the first few words that came out of her mouth.

Mohit’s face looked confused and a bit shocked. He then turned to his father, “Tau’s shop? As what?”

"We will discuss that with your uncle. Maybe he will decide. For now, you can just sit at his shop and observe how everyone works there, greet the customers, and sell clothes.", his father intervened before Sita could utter the next few words, "Your Tau feels it will be a good start for you. Your mother and I feel the same way."

Mohit looks back at his mother as she turns her gaze away from him. He takes a bite out of his breakfast, knowing that silence was the only response he could give. His father was not going to budge given Mohit's performance in his exams.

"Okay…" he said. Sita realised her son's disappointment but they all knew it was for the best.

The morning had ended on a quiet note. Shraddha, her younger daughter rushed for school with her father. Mohit went back to his room.

The clock had struck half past 2. Sita washed the dishes quietly in the kitchen. She packed away the rotis, the shape of which took her back by 22 years.

"You have taught your daughter well. She makes a good cup of tea. What about your rotis? Do they come out round or the shape of America?"

Her mind wandered back to the days when she met Amit for the first time. She still remembered the twinkle in his smile while his mother asked Sita jokingly about her ability to make perfectly round rotis.

"I don't mind if the rotis are the shape of America." Amit was charming as ever.

Today, that glimmer of love seemed to have taken the side road. With life's struggles and working hard to put bread on the table, Amit was worried all the time.

"Our son, Amit, has a government job. So, you don't have to worry about your daughter's well-being. After all, we are now Sita's parents and not just her in-laws."

Wiping the kitchen table top, Sita wonders how Amit was burdened with the family's expenses over the years. His parents believed that it was the son's sole responsibility to earn while the daughter-in-law managed the family and raised the children.

As Sita was done with her work in the kitchen, she went to her children's room. Mohit was asleep on his bed next to the window. The sun shined harshly on his face. She walked towards the window, drew the curtains, and switched on the table fan next to him.

Sita gave a long look at him. All decisions, be it the school they went to, the clothes they wore, the friends they made, and anything else, were always decided for them. A sinking feeling settled in her gut as she realised, it had been the same with her for 40 years of her life. Since she was born to this very day, all decisions were made on her behalf. The only time Sita truly felt alive was when she managed the house.

It was when the line of control was stretched for her to make independent decisions, of course, not without consulting her husband and in-laws. But most times, he would not want to be burdened with home affairs. So, a lot was left to Sita, from when the kids went out to play or to the movies they would watch with their friends, and so on.

Fifteen years later, Sita still felt the need to always look at her husband before either saying a word or making major decisions. Why was it always that way? Why did dancing in the rain without an umbrella, visiting an old friend, or taking that morning walk in solitude feel more like freedom compared to her life?

Sita wondered what the missing link was… It wasn't like Amit kept her locked up in the house. He did support her many times. He took care of the kids whenever Sita needed to visit her parents. He helped the children with their homework when she was unwell while also cooking the food for her despite his mother's disagreement with his actions.

Indeed, obeying her in-laws was an unspoken rule. She remembered the other time that she'll never forget. The younger adults were not allowed to take an afternoon nap. Of course, this rule mainly applied to Sita.

"Sita… Sita? Get up, someone is at the door. Go see who it is." Sita goes back to the time when she would try to catch a wink in the afternoon. There was hardly a moment's rest from morning to noon. She would manage to scrape in an hour's rest before the kids would come home from school. Some years, Mohit went to school in the afternoon while Shraddha went in the morning. The hours were erratic, not to mention making sure her father-in-law took his medicines.

"Arrey, leave your slippers. Just listen to that incessant ringing of the bell? Go fast." Said her mother-in-law.

Rubbing the sleep off her eyes, Sita managed to balance her footsteps across the hallway. The mailman looked curiously at Sita for taking so long to open the door.

"Next time, don't sleep in the afternoon. What will happen if someone is at the door? Your father-in-law's and my sleep get disrupted. You are young now, there's no need to take an afternoon nap while my son is working hard at his government job."

Never a day went by in all those years when her mother-in-law would not emphasise the fact that her son worked at a government post. It was like a label on the front door of the Trivedi household.

Well, those years went by and Sita still thinks to this day about the number of restrictions laid on her. She loved being a homemaker but what she didn't understand was why everyone made her feel less for it. She took respite in the fact that Amit hardly ever made her feel so, but the years of working hard and struggling with expenses did sometimes push him over the edge.

Gradually as Sita looked back at the years of her married life, she started to feel that the problem was not in her being a homemaker or being a working mother, it was her deed of renouncing the power to make decisions. Why should all the decision-making fall only in the hands of one spouse while no one else's opinion is welcomed?

Would it be the same for her children? Of course, times have changed but have Mohit and Shraddha grown up with a mindset conditioned to be extremely subservient to what their family said? Would that be good for them in the long run?

PART 2

Just then her doorbell rang. At half past 2, who could be at the door?

Curious to know who it may be, she quickly walked toward the main door.

"Oh, Sheetal! Such a long time. Come, come."

"I was worried whether you would recognise me after all these years." Sheetal removed her shoes outside the door and walked in. Sita welcomed her old neighbour who shifted 10 years ago from the same colony where they lived.

"It's been so long! How have you been? How are Rohan and the kids?"

The two ladies continued to talk while Sita took Sheetal into the kitchen while she prepared some tea. Mohit was still asleep in his room. Sita had an underlying thought wondering why Sheetal had come to visit her after 10 years out of the blue. Her sudden visit was a surprise and concern. Was everything all right…? She thought to herself.

"Wow, you were the third or fourth tenant to move into this colony, right?" Sita asked as she tried to slowly inch her way to the main question.

"The third actually, yes." Sheetal agreed, "I mean, it had been almost fourteen or fifteen years till we finally moved out. We knew it was time."

"Yes, but it all happened so fast. Suddenly, one day you showed up at my door with two suitcases telling me that you were leaving for good. God knows how many more suitcases you had placed down the building already. And that's it, we thought that was the last day we'd see you… but I am glad you kept in touch on WhatsApp. You were still in our lady's colony group."

"Yes, I didn't want to lose touch with anyone. After all, I have known all of you for so long. We spent so many good times together."

Sita and Sheetal talked about the years gone by and what their respective children were doing. There was so much to talk about that neither of them knew where to start.

"If it's okay," Sita interjected, "why did you leave all of a sudden? I mean, I hope you don't mind. I just thought that it's not my place to ask so I didn't press further on it but still… None of the ladies wanted to pry so they didn't ask you directly in the chat group either. Was everything all right back then?"

"I understand. Anyone would be curious. Honestly, we did not know what to tell everyone so we just kept it under wraps." Sheetal paused as though letting herself go back in time. "We were going through some financial difficulties. With Rohan's salary and my earnings put together, the children's school fees, the maintenance bills, our car insurance, and so many expenses, it started to get overwhelming for us. I mean, how many times could we take a loan or ask for money from relatives? Rohan and I would have several discussions together. A few months later, we made a conscious decision to move out and into a smaller apartment… you know, just until we could regain our financial standing. At that time, we believed it would be the right decision."

"Oh, was it that bad?"

"It had not yet gotten to that point but it would have in a year or two. We had to think for both the children. It was a tough decision but then we had to make it and I am glad we did."

"So, you, Rohan, and the kids moved where exactly? I mean, in the same town?"

"Yes, in the same city, of course. But at that time, we lived in a small one-bedroom apartment two hours away from here. It was unlike the two-bedroom flat we had in this society."

Sita drank her cup of tea as she listened intently to Sheetal.

"Eventually, Rohan and I saved enough money that we could have moved to a better apartment. But we decided not to as we still wanted to save more for the future of our kids, their studies, and our retirement. To be honest, we developed the habit of saving more than spending without thinking, and we also got used to where we were living."

"So, do you still live there?"

"Yes, for now, we still live in the same locality but in a bigger apartment. I think we made a good decision because the expenses are also less. It worked out for us. See, sometimes, there are adjustments but for the future, I think we need to be aware of our expenses in the present."

Sita was overwhelmed with the thought of the several adjustments her old neighbour had to make but a glimmer of hope set in her eyes.

"So, how did you and Rohan plan these things? It's nice to see that you both made decisions together."

"Of course, he and I always discussed these things together. Sita, this would not have worked if Rohan was uptight about his finances. I mean, at that time, I was working at a very low pay in my previous job, so you can imagine how he must have felt burdened with the majority of the expenses."

"So, have you saved enough? I mean, for you and Rohan's retirement? For the kid's studies?"

"We have saved enough and we are continuing to save as best we can. I would not say that we have completely accomplished our goals, but yes, ten years of saving and planning every expense has made a huge difference for our family. Who knew cutting down on spending would help us realise how unnecessary some expenses were? Also, it got better with our increasing incomes."

She paused again and then said, "It was easy for us to make tough decisions because we knew what was at stake, our livelihood and the well-being of our children. But, at the same time, it was difficult to explain to the children. They were still too young to understand. But, over time, we educated them about the reality of our situation. We also taught them how to calculate monthly expenses and compare them annually. Today, our kids have grown so much because of it that now they tell us how we should and should not spend it!"

The conversation continued for another two hours. Sheetal left but promised that she would visit Sita again with her husband and kids.

For a moment, Sita started to feel hopeful for her son. She thought that whether or not Mohit worked at his uncle's shop, continued his studies, or did both together, what mattered was teaching them the right way to manage their money for a secure future.

Sita knew it was time to educate herself on the experience her old neighbour shared with her. Only then could she influence a better change and future for her family.

PART 3

A few weeks later…

"Smells good in here." inhaling the aroma of cardamom in the kitchen, "Is that the new chai you bought yesterday?"

Amit turned, a little smile crinkling the corners of his eyes, "Yes, it is. Do you want me to pour you a cup?"

"I wouldn't mind one, yes," Sita replied, taking a seat at the table, hardly feeling any hint of an evening breeze. As Amit poured the tea, Sita noticed the worry lines permanently etched on his forehead softening slightly.

To draw Amit into a conversation, Sita was prepared to make her case. Breathing in the memories of the past few weeks, she tried remembering the lines she would use to convince him.

She had realised that it was not just enough to live for each day but to also think and plan for the future. She no longer wanted to see her husband burdened by the weight of expenses. It was time she intervened but how and what were going to be her next steps, she wondered.

The best person to reach out to was the old neighbour who visited her a few weeks ago. She was the only one who could help Sita decide what to do next. After a week of unending phone calls with Sheetal, while also visiting her personally, Sita was equipped with a rough roadmap of what to do next.

The weekend approached, and the Trivedi household was finally settling into new beginnings of Mohit going to work. Shraddha was reading a novel on the rug in the living room.

Taking a sip from the cup "Our evening tea time should always be like this, isn't it? You and I are sitting together on the weekend in the evenings."

"Brings back old memories right before we got married. When we met once at that Irani café. Remember? It was the same, quiet evening."

"Where did those days go?" Sita asked Amit

She smiled at him, waiting for her cue.

There was a long pause between the two of them. Amit sat, drinking his tea, reminiscing about the old days while Sita looked for the opportunity to jump in, and finally…

"I was thinking about Mohit."

Amit skipped a smile, "Is everything all right?"

"Yes, yes, everything's fine." She reassured him, "It's just… how is he doing at work?"

"Rajesh bhai said he is doing okay, seems a bit uninterested but since Monday, he has been taking some initiative. He is training him to keep track of the sales and inventory."

"That's good." Sita took a sip of tea, allowing the silence to stretch for a moment, "You know how you said that with his graduation marks, he may not get a good job? We don't know what will happen in the future but we can plan for it now, right?"

In the living room where Shraddha sat, reading the same book, she could hear what her mother was talking about. Her attention quickly shifted to her parents in the kitchen.

Amit set his cup down with a sigh, "What do you mean?"

"Remember Sheetal, our old neighbour? She visited us last week?"

A flicker of recognition crossed Amit's face, "Hmm… yes, I remember."

"Well," Sita continued, "Do you know why they moved away suddenly all those years ago?"

Amit shook his head.

"They were having some money problems."

"Oh, how come? They both had jobs."

"Yes but it was not enough. They were still struggling to lead a good life. And that is what got me thinking, Amit. You have been doing this all on your own. Paying the bills, expenses of the medical treatments, and so much… How did you manage?"

"It is not easy but I think I am better at doing this than Sheetal and Rohan."

Sita, almost rolling her eyes, "Uh... yes, that's my point! You did so well all by yourself... But..." taking a deep breath, she continues, "Do we want our children to go through what you have been through all these years? Mohit should not suffer in silence the way you did, trying to manage all the expenses by himself. Shraddha, living like me, always waiting for someone to decide on her behalf?"

"Oh, so you think that I have not done a good job? You think I am suffering in silence?" Amit looks at Sita, puzzled, "I did everything I could for this family. It's not easy but all you can see is what we lack. If you have to only complain about everything then why are you sitting here having tea with me. I should have known something was up with you. Always stirring something in your head."

Shraddha's eyes deviate from the book and focus on the kitchen table where she sees her father's hand holding the thin porcelain tea cup.

"That's not what I meant, Amit. You have done so much for all of us. What I am saying is that you should not have had to do it all alone. Wouldn't it have been better if you had some help to..."

"Enough! I thought we could have a good time drinking tea peacefully. But you have other things to discuss."

Leaving his cup half empty on the table, Amit walks out of the kitchen. Shraddha, noticing her parents just had an argument, glues her eyes back into the book. Her father walked past her angrily where his eye somehow caught the title of the book Shraddha was reading - *One Day At A Time*.

Sita sat back in her chair, sighing as she wondered why her perspective was barely considered over the years.

The weekend had passed with another bout of silence, eclipsing the Trivedi household. There seemed to have been no room for a conversation unless someone was at the door or the TV had to be switched on or off. Sita and Amit were not talking to each other, giving quick glances so as to not get in each other's way, especially in the bedroom. Sita folded the clothes and put them in the cupboard. Amit was reading a message on his mobile.

Just then, they hear a loud thud. Shraddha screams in agony. Amit and Sita follow the scream and rush to the living room. They can't find Shraddha, although her painful moans were definitely coming from the living room. Finally, Sita looks at the floor, barely noticing Shraddha's hand behind the sofa.

She runs towards Shraddha and Amit follows her. They try to help Shradha get up, finding that she can barely stand on her feet. "Her ankle is swollen, Sita. We will have to take her to the hospital. Call a cab, I will put her on the sofa here."

Sita grabs her purse from the room and runs out of the house to hail a taxi. Meanwhile Amit is sitting with Shraddha on the sofa, "What happened? How did you fall?"

In her state of agony, she manages to say, "I slipped."

Three days later, Amit and Sita bring Shraddha home in a wheelchair with her left leg plastered. Mohit and Sita help Shraddha settle on the bed. She immediately falls asleep.

Later, Sita and Mohit sit with Amit in the living room. Amit's father and mother are also sitting with them waiting to understand what the doctor said. Using a kerchief to wipe the sweat from his forehead, "2 Lakhs plus the hospital charges. This is the third fixed deposit account I have broken this year."

"Ask money from Rajesh" Amit's father intervenes, "he will lend some money."

"I already owe him a lot, papa. I won't ask anymore now."

The same eclipsed silence takes over with only the ceiling fan oscillating above their heads.

"He is your elder brother. There is nothing to be embarrassed about…"

"Baba, please. Just let me sit here and rest. It's been three long agonising days running out and around the hospital. We should put a carpet behind the sofa, somehow, the floor there is too polished or it's like a blind spot."

In the past three days, Amit and Sita started talking again. The argument they had at the kitchen table felt less significant compared to their daughter's pain and surgery to treat her fracture.

The people at the bank looked at Amit in disappointment and worry. It was his third fixed deposit in the same year. Sita noticed how worried Amit had become when he had to again part with money he took several years to grow. It was over in a moment's notice.

Three days later when they finally brought Shraddha home, the air was filled with relief. This time, her in-laws, Amit and Mohit were all together.

"Why don't we set up an emergency fund?"

Amit looks at Sita, "Now what is all this about?"

"An emergency fund… instead of you breaking your fixed deposit every time… we could…"

"You think I have not thought about that? To do that we have to have money that is worth a minimum of three to six months of our expenses. We barely have any after breaking three deposits. There's just one last one left in the bank now."

An Emergency Fund is a financial safety net that people create through banks to safeguard money for major unexpected costs, legal fees, or travel emergencies.

"But if we start something, say next month, can we not achieve a certain amount?"

"How do you know what an emergency fund is? Have you been talking to Sheetal again?"

"Well…" Sita fumbles "With Rohan also…"

Amit stares at Sita.

She hesitates, and then reveals, "and with their financial advisor… also…"

"What are you doing when I am at work all day? Now I know why the phone bill was so high last month."

"Arrey, you stop getting angry all the time," Sita finally had some help from her mother-in-law, "Allow bahu to say what she wants to say. Yes, Sita, what were you saying?"

"Thank you, sasu ma." Sita takes a deep breath, "see, if we use a separate account and add a little money every month in an emergency account. Some from you and some from Mohit. It will provide some relief in the future." She looks at everyone in the living room. Mohit looks intently at his mother. Amit is looking at the floor processing whatever Sita was saying while also calming himself down.

Her father-in-law and mother-in-law looked seriously at Sita trying to understand what she was saying, "Also, the fixed deposit you broke, Amit. While paying the hospital bill, you told me that we have a balance of Rs 5 lakhs from that account. We can either let the five lakhs accumulate in a renewed fixed deposit or we add that also to the emergency funds account. I mean, this is just a suggestion. The rest, you will know better."

An FD or Fixed Deposit is an account that you can open in the bank to deposit a lump sum amount for a fixed period. After the fixed period, such as three or six months to a year, and so on, is completed, the returns from this deposit are higher based on a predetermined interest rate.

In Sita and Amit's case, they could open an FD or divide the balance of five lakhs in the emergency fund account as well.

They could use the FD to:

- Accumulate wealth

- Continue to make short-term investments
- Add the returns to the emergency account
- Make the FD part of the retirement savings by building a corpus of funds

To my Courage readers…
Share a moment in your life where you took the courage to change the course of a decision… something you are proud of!!
Share your story by scanning this QR Code

Almost a minute had passed. Amit was still looking at the floor thinking hard... Stroking his hair and rubbing his tired eyes, he stands up…

“Maybe we can do something.”

A wave of relief washed over Sita. Surprised at what he said, Sita smiled, knowing that his acknowledgement could be the start of a better future for her children.

“We could divide the expenses also… Mohit, from now on, you pay the electricity bill and quarterly maintenance bill. Let’s start from there… and now I am going for a shower, I am really tired. Sita, are there any more surprises you have hidden?”

Sita smiles at Amit with a hint of hope in her eyes.

“Don’t answer that question…” Amit quickly walks away.

PART 4

Over the days and months that passed, there was more clarity on the money coming in and going out from the Trivedi Household. Sita would learn with Amit about the specific ways to save money. He had divided the five lakh rupees equally, adding one part to a new fixed deposit and the other half to an emergency fund to account for a higher yield.

Rs 5,00,000*	
Emergency Fund	**Fixed Deposit**
Rs 2,50,000*	**Rs 2,50,000***
You can use an emergency fund (a swipe in FD) if you prioritise liquidity and require easy access during emergencies.	You can use a fixed deposit if you are willing to hold off the liquidity for higher potential returns.
Interest rates are generally lower but are designed to be highly liquid where you can access money quickly.	Committing your money for a fixed period, so you typically get offered higher interest rates on returns.
**The amounts used above are representational and pertain to this story. You can decide the quantities you wish to grow through an emergency or a fixed deposit account based on your financial strategy.*	

Amit also taught his son how to save a certain sum from his income every month. So, Mohit would get Rs 15,000 every month from which he would save Rs 9000 and keep aside. By the end of 12 months, he saved One Lakh and Eight Thousand Rupees. His father asked him to divide his savings equally in a new fixed deposit account and a mutual funds account.

Rs 1,08,000*	
Mohit saved in a year: Rs 9,000 x 12 months (out of his salary of Rs 15,000 per month) = Rs 1,08,000. He equally divided his savings into a fixed deposit and mutual funds account.	
Mutual Fund	**Fixed Deposit**
Rs 54,000*	**Rs 54,000***
You can invest this money in a variety of securities, such as stocks, bonds, or a combination of both. The goal is to provide you with diversified	You can use a fixed deposit if you are willing to hold off the liquidity for higher potential returns.

exposure to the market and professional management.	
You can invest in different types of mutual funds including: · Equity Funds: Invest primarily in stocks. · Bond Funds: Invest primarily in bonds. · Balanced Funds: Invest in a mix of stocks and bonds. · Index Funds: Track a specific market index, such as the S&P 500. · Sector Funds: Focus on a particular industry or sector.	The core concept of a fixed deposit remains the same. However, there can be variations in terms: · Tenure: Fixed deposits can have varying terms, ranging from a few months to several years. Longer tenures often come with higher interest rates. · Interest Frequency: Interest can be paid monthly, quarterly, half-yearly, or annually. The frequency can impact your overall returns. · Interest Calculation: Interest can be calculated on a simple interest or compound interest basis. Compound interest generally yields higher returns over time. · Premature Withdrawal Penalties: Many fixed deposits have penalties for early withdrawal. These penalties can vary depending on the bank and the tenure. · Auto-Renewal: Some fixed deposits can be set up for auto-renewal, where the maturity amount is automatically reinvested in a new fixed deposit.
**The amounts used above are representational and pertain to this story. Based on your financial strategy, you can decide the quantities you wish to grow through a mutual fund or a fixed deposit account.*	

Below are the differences in returns among different streams based on a one-time 2 Lakh investment for the next 30 years.

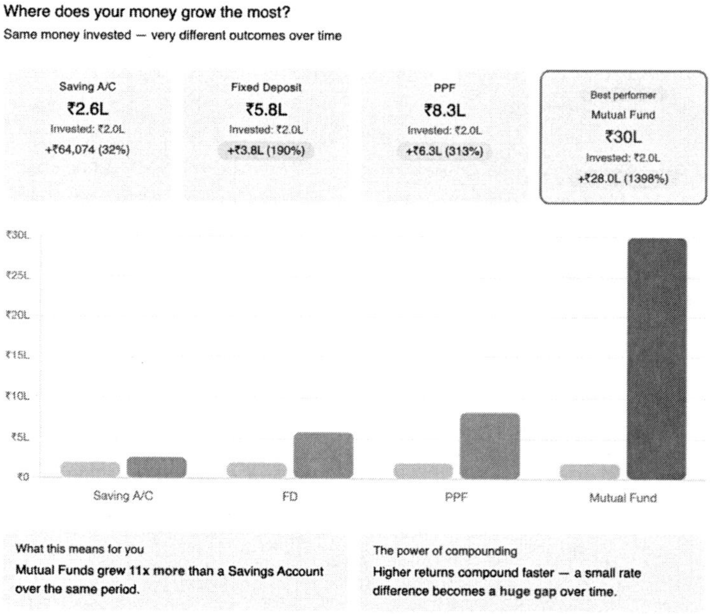

Meanwhile, Mohit and Shraddha decided to maintain a year log book to track their expenses.

- They bought new clothing, like once in a quarter, and only after comparing prices online and from local clothing vendors.
- I made sure to have more home-cooked food and ate outside only once a month.
- They used less electricity, especially when not needed.
- Sita bought bulk groceries which were cheaper compared to buying a little every day.

A few deliberate but reasonable adjustments here and there helped the Trivedi family build up emergency funds, while also saving money overall. Reducing expenses was not easy but they gradually learnt how to differentiate between an important and a non-crucial expense. Seeing their family wealth increasing one day at a time was truly satisfying.

"Maintaining an emergency funds account is not easy. There's always something that happens and we have to spend that money. It's been three years now, and we have already withdrawn Three lakhs from that account." Amit tells his brother, Rajesh.

"How much is left in that account?"

"We have now some Two and half lakhs."

"Okay, so do one thing. Split the money into two separate emergency funds right now."

"Two? Maintaining one is so difficult." Amit complained. "The money just gets spent, either on Baba's medicines or our mother's treatment. Last year, I had a leg injury, so I asked Sita to withdraw from our emergency fund account for urgent treatment. The surgeon charged us one Lakh for it."

"Yes, that is exactly why you should make more than one emergency account. Otherwise, at this rate, you will end up breaking your fixed deposits also."

Amit ponders aloud, "We have managed to generate at least six lakhs in two fixed deposits, and 7.5 lakhs in mutual funds. We are building up some allocated funds for Shraddha's future studies. And the rest till Mohit's retirement."

"That is good. See, Amit, nobody said saving for the future would be easy. It never is but at the end the rewards you and your wife will reap for yourselves and your children will all be worth it. In fact, it's been five years since you started saving, don't you feel that by the end of another twenty years, you and your family are set for life?"

Amit nods in approval, thinking what more he could do to increase the family wealth. He knew that the one thing he required was patience and consistency in saving habits. He was planning on lending a flat for rent which would fetch him additional income for the family. However, he knew that to put a flat on rent, he would need lakhs of rupees for flats away from the city. However, he would need Crores of rupees for one within the city.

A few days went by wondering what he could do.

“My mother had given me this jewellery on our wedding day. She said that we could sell it and use the money during emergencies.” Sita showed Amit a bag of gold ornaments from bangles to earrings, necklaces. “Why don’t we get them weighed and priced so that we can use it to buy a flat?”

Amit looked into the bag. It was filled with different types of gold ornaments. He could feel the weight of it in his hands. “But this is all your gold given by your mother. Are you okay parting with it?”

Sita smiled at Amit, “What do you think this gold was given to me for? During times like these when we needed to build our wealth. Let’s go to the gold shop and ask them how much we could get from it.”

The following day, Amit and Sita were at the gold shop. The man in the shop weighed all the gold and gave them a fair price of Rs 15 lakhs. This includes the gold that Amit and Sita had also bought over the years.

“It’s not much for buying a flat. We will have to think of something else.” Said Amit. “Also, we can’t sell all the gold. It is our major family asset.”

“What if we put some into our existing fixed deposits and let it grow until we can use the money to buy a flat?” Sita was curious

“That might take a long time and over the years, property prices inflate.” Amit started to think deeper, “Maybe it’s not possible to put a flat on rent.”

Meanwhile the man at the gold shop overheard their conversation, “Just use the rent-to-own or lease-to-own option. You don’t have to buy a property by paying all at once. That way, you can pay the full amount in parts for a specified period.”

Amit and Sita realised that they may have been underestimating their options. "That's a good idea," said Amit. "But we need to look further into it. Do you have someone who can give us some guidance?" He asked the gold shop owner.

"My elder brother has dealt with all these things. He has put many flats on rent and it's not like he had all the money ready in-hand to pay for these flats." The show owner takes out a piece of paper and writes a number on it. "My brother's name is Jignesh bhai. This is his mobile number. Tell him Pragnesh bhai gave you his number and you need some guidance on putting flats on rent."

Over the next six months, Amit and Sita were on a couple's adventure researching flats to put on rent. After several talks with Jignesh bhai, they were able to understand the way ahead for owning or renting a flat, and subletting them. From one bedroom to two! Meanwhile, they sold some gold worth Rs 10 lakhs and allowed a part of it to grow in a fixed deposit account for a year while they put some in a mutual fund for the same period. This helped them grow their money from Rs 10 lakhs to Rs 20 lakhs.

Once they grew the money, they were able to buy a flat through a rent-to-own option. This way, Amit and Sita were able to get additional income through rent while also paying off the remaining money for the flat.

Ten more years had passed while the family had continued to build on their savings. In a total of fifteen years, the Trivedi household was filled not with too many items or new wall paints but with the relief of a secure future. Their assets had increased along with the readiness for emergencies. "But I am thinking about the years that have gone by. We have not gone on a vacation anywhere. All we've done is go to our maasi's place or visit a beach nearby. It's hardly anything. I think we are putting off too many things for the future." Sita said.

"You are right. I am mostly concerned about the sudden emergencies that we have to face. Papa's medical needs. My leg injury that happened years ago. I don't want such accidents to happen and then we are back to square one."

As a reader, can you start your Emergency fund right now?	Amount (min 20% of the income)	Bank/FD Account
This month		
Month 2		
Month 3		
Month 4		
Month 5		
Month 6		
Month 7		
Month 8		
Month 9		
Month 10		
Continue …….		
Total (till you accumulate 3 months expenses)		

Need the help of a financial consultant to help build an emergency fund?

Scan this code to join my community.

Let's continue…

"Do you remember about the time I attended that food hall exhibition? There was a lady there by the name Bhavani who told me about the travel packages she books so that she and her family can enjoy a good family vacation. It doesn't even cost her too much compared to other touring packages."

"But it's not just the tour package cost. We will have to consider the money we need for eating, lodging, buying things, if at all."

"I think the travel package may include everything. Amit, it's been a long time and as a family we have done nothing but save and save. I think a once-in-a-while trip, 15 years, to be precise, deserves at least one vacation. Can you plan an itinerary and budget your holiday? Food, local travel, Stay, and to and fro tickets…. Of course, some shopping will add more to the excitement."

Amit reflects on the years gone by. He sees how hard his son has worked to build his career, the income he generates has increased from 15,000 a month to 150,000 a month. He sees how Shraddha has a job now. Her earnings have also started to fuel their savings, which will reduce after she gets married but he is less worried about the future now.

"Okay, let's go somewhere, all four of us. Let's pick a week and hopefully, it should not clash with Mohit's or Shraddha's work, and neither with my work."

> Saving for the years that come does not mean that you have to sacrifice all the fun times that you can have with near and dear ones. Saving and managing expenses also means that you navigate expenses and enjoy life responsibly without any meaningless expenses. That's just what Amit and Sita did as they realised that savings and investing in the future can take decades. It would not be wise to simply enjoy the fruits of their labour only after they cross age 60.

A few years later, Amit decided to retire from his job. Mohit was married and so was Shraddha. The family had come full circle as they made wiser decisions when it came to family and future planning. The family assets had grown from making 7 lakhs a year to 40 lakhs a year from their combined earnings, fixed deposits, and mutual funds, not to mention, the two sublets they had managed to build together over a span of 20 years.

“Make a wish first.” Mohit said to his father as Sita, Shraddha, her husband, and Mohit’s wife with their firstborn stood over a cake that read - ‘*The Journey has just Begun*’.

It was Amit’s retirement party that they held at home as a small ceremony to mark the completion of their father's years of hard work and dedication towards his family. A quiet celebration after the dinner table was wiped clean. Amit gave the first bite to Sita, and then to everyone else.

A while later, Sita had arranged the kitchen table for some tea.

“At this time?”

“Just for the two of us. Our little ceremony. After all, this is the table where it all began. Our dreams about an uncertain future. Now, we’ve achieved what we wanted to achieve. A good future for our children and for us.”

“What are you talking about?” Amit smiled, “There’s still so much to do. Places to go. Our journey has just begun, Sita.”

She smiled back at Amit as she sipped her cup of tea.

Overall, the Trivedi family's financial journey involved a combination of disciplined savings, strategic investments, and informed decision-making. Their efforts led to a strong financial foundation and a brighter future.

Financial Steps:

- **Emergency Fund Creation:** Established an emergency fund to cover unexpected expenses.
- **Budgeting and Expense Tracking:** Implemented a system to track income and expenses, identifying areas for savings.
- **Debt Reduction:** Focused on paying off existing debts, such as credit card balances.
- **Investment Diversification:** Spread investments across various assets like fixed deposits, mutual funds, and real estate.

- **Financial Education:** Sought advice from financial experts and learned about personal finance concepts.
- **Lifestyle Changes:** Adopted better habits, such as cooking at home, reducing unnecessary expenses, and buying in bulk.

Assets Gained:

- **Emergency Fund:** Built a substantial emergency fund to cover unexpected financial challenges.
- **Fixed Deposits:** Accumulated funds in fixed deposits for steady returns.
- **Mutual Funds:** Invested in mutual funds for potential growth and diversification.
- **Real Estate:** Acquired a rental property for passive income.
- **Financial Knowledge:** Gained a deeper understanding of personal finance principles and strategies.
- **Peace of Mind:** Experienced reduced financial stress and increased security for the future.

One-Minute Financial Hack!!!

Here's a little trick to make sure you save without knowing it...

Car key Jar – Every time you misplace the car/vehicle key, pay the Jar Rs 50 . (This way both keys are safe or savings are increased.)

Book Club Chats

- What did you think about Amit's personality? How did his understanding of family finances and partnership evolve throughout the story?
- Should Sita have pursued employment to bring additional income, or was her contribution as a homemaker equally valuable? How did her role change even without formal employment?
- What other financial strategies might have helped the Trivedi family achieve their goals faster or more effectively?
- How did cultural expectations around gender roles impact the financial decisions in the Trivedi household?
- What moment in the story do you consider the true turning point in Sita and Amit's relationship?

Potential Roadblocks: How to Handle?

1. **Social commitments:** A far away relative's wedding / events etc:

   Potential resolution: Use the emergency fund temporarily and refill the same in some time period.
2. **Medical Emergencies:** Get your Mediclaim done for the family too.
3. **Need in business:** Create boundaries on how much can be invested in business from personal funds.

Rathandeep's Kaleidoscope

Life can be colourful when together. Earning is not important, directing and executing is!!! Celebrate small wins with focus on key goals. One day at a time is the theme of the story, everyday decisions on finances have a great impact on the goals we can achieve. Start early like Sheetal and have the freedom for a beautiful life .

Back in the garden

“Wow” Geetha said, “You really pulled it together for your family, Sita. It’s great that you had a husband who was so supportive. Not every wife has that luxury.”

“Well, it was not easy. Through the years, Amit and I learnt to understand each other. We had our disagreements but somehow managed to settle it because we knew that we were headed in the right direction.”

Everybody smiled at Sita, adoring her spirit and resilient faith in her family.

“So, who wants to go next?” Meetha looked around and asked, “Geetha? I think you too had a difficult time convincing your husband. How did it all start?”

“Oh” Geetha rolled her eyes, “I was in a real pickle. Over the years, I realised the mountain was in my head. I thought status meant everything until I realised what people were not talking about. So, here’s how it all started…”

A HIGH SOCIETY WEDDING, A TAUNT, AND A FINANCIAL PLAN

PART 1

"Don't tell me where I should stand. I am a senior citizen. You should have that much sense."

"You can't just break the line from here. Please go to the back of the line. I am asking nicely because of your age."

"Hey, you watch your mouth."

The photographer turned his camera away from the bride and groom, taking clear shots of the slurs that burst like firecrackers in the air. The meet and greet line at Rohan and Avni's wedding had grown from a single line to a cluster group of angry people.

Family members of the bride and groom rushed to the scene. Rohan and Avni were about to get off stage to make sure everything was all right but they hesitated with confused anticipation. Jatin and the old man wouldn't quit arguing. Geetha tried to calm Jatin, telling him to let it go. However, even if he did, it was clear that his newly met queue breaker would not stand down.

Geetha would have never predicted this flow of events, a rather grievous disruption. Would her husband and a known relative of the bride's side get into a verbal fistfight? Not a clue. The argument had reached high decibels until Rohan and Avni had to step off the stage to douse off the fire, while their parents arranged for cold water for the raging opponents.

"Don't misbehave. Have your parents taught you nothing?"

"Uncle, you don't need to tell me anything. Watch what you are doing."

"Who do you think you are calling *uncle*?"

"You said it, you are a senior citizen!!"

The raised voices did not permit Geetha to utter a single word. Even if she tried to say something to calm Jatin, would she say it loud enough?

Just a while ago, everything was normal. The day had started with the blessings of their GPS guiding them to the right location. *Rohan Jain weds Avni Kataria*, "There's the board." Jatin gestures at a poster elegantly painted outside the wedding hall as he turns the steering wheel to the right and parks the car.

Saakshi and Diya are decked up for the wedding. Jatin, his parents and Geetha step out of the car. The mother-in-law checks both girls' dresses as they leave the car, "Good, nothing is crumpled. Be good inside, okay girls! No running around."

"Haan, Daadi," Saakshi says, holding her grandmother's hand

Jatin holds Diya's hand while Geetha checks herself thoroughly, from her hair to her dupatta, hoping nothing on her is out of place.

They enter the hall and view all the decorations. As though walking into a palace of grandeur, the family felt like they hadn't dressed well enough for the occasion. "Looks like we underestimated Maami's comment when she said Rohan's in-laws are super rich," Jatin looked around the hall. Waiters served water and handed napkins to the elderly. There were designated servers, specially assigned to give a handful of flowers to each guest for the blessing ceremony during the seven rounds around the sacred fire.

The ceremonies went on, where the bride, the groom, and their parents were seated together around the sacred fire. Relatives met each other, talking about how the bride looked stunning and the groom looked smart in his sherwani.

The wedding was followed by the reception. Geetha and Jatin proceeded to the buffet hall. It started with the distribution of clean, empty plates to the snacks stall followed by salads, starters, and the vegetarian buffet, and finally the sweets and other delectables. Geetha followed with the kids and their grandmother while the line behind them started getting longer.

"Do you know how much they have spent on this wedding?" a close relative sat next to Jatin and Geetha at a table. He was popularly called the 'Gossip Uncle' but was tolerated only because the information he had was always true. "42 Lakhs!"

Jatin's mother almost choked on the papad she was eating.

Geetha makes an effort to talk. Her voice always stayed below human decibels, low-toned and hesitant, "Really, 42…"

Before anyone could hear her voice in the crowded food hall.

"42 Lakhs?" Jatin questioned

Geetha found herself at the mercy of a conversation like it always had been where she played the timid spectator. Her introvertedness sometimes would catch a person off-guard when they would finally realise that she was in the same room. Geetha lived a quiet life growing up. Her father inherited a decent bungalow from his parents which gave his family a roof of quiet shelter in the outskirts of a city. But his job as an electrician paid for bread on the table while her mother provided tuition for her neighbourhood kids. Growing up, Geetha learnt the hard way of depriving herself of the things she liked only because of the lack of money. When she married Jatin, she lived still as though she were deprived, in conversation and lifestyle.

"Yes, but you know how it is…" said the gossip uncle, "weddings cost more at times. Imagine how much they have spent on the guests who are coming from out of town. They have given them accommodation in a nearby hotel."

"But they have a younger daughter also, right? So, now will they have enough money to spend on her wedding?" Jatin grew more and more curious.

"They own multiple businesses. They can manage, they just don't show it. But today, look at the decorations and the number of waiters, the caterers, so much food, and even the dresses they are wearing, everything looks so expensive."

Geetha looked around, noticing how everyone was having a great time. She saw the same people take two more rounds at the buffet stall. Her gaze fell upon the six-foot-tall flower pots placed in all six corners. The ice sculptor that was shaped in the form of the bride and groom in the middle was placed on the table surrounded by an assortment of salads. She remembered the gold-glittered artificial rose flower they gave each of them with a '*Thank You for Coming*' note when they entered the hall in the morning. The guests were treated with royalty unlike she had ever seen at other weddings.

"Oh, this Jalebi and Rabdi are amazing. Just try it, don't forget. I am going to take another one. Save my seat here." *Gossip uncle* went for another round.

A wave of anxiety clouded Geetha's mind, recalling the day of her wedding to Jatin ten years ago. What she would wear, how she would look. The minor thought of applying a dash of eye shadow rattled her senses. *'You didn't get it done professionally? Your mole can still be seen. It's okay, you look good dear. Don't worry!'* She remembers a relative's snide remarks like it was yesterday. The so-called compliments were etched into her brain, *'Oh, Geetha, you are looking bloated even on your wedding day. At least for a few months, you could have resisted those delicious biryanis your mother makes. Anyway, you still look good despite all the extra baggage. So, should I stand next to you for the photo?'* Relatives always believed in crossing the line.

Brought back to the present, she realised the time had arrived for taking a photo with the bride and groom. She could not help but maintain a nervous smile, unable to make eye contact with Rohan and Avni. Jatin, with his mother and daughter Saakshi stood next to Rohan while Geetha took Diya beside her and stood next to Avni.

"Ready? Clicking…" The photographer takes a couple of photos while noticing the half smiles, "Done"

Before they knew it, Geetha and her family left the wedding. It was the most awkward walk towards the exit. Their thoughts screamed louder as Geetha walked out with her family. Just then she heard an unknown relative standing close by, mumbling, and as she got closer, the words became clearer "*They must not be often invited to high-society weddings.*"

Were the words meant for her family, for the line-breaker, or both? She wondered in quiet anxiety and shame.

"Yes, okay… okay… no, I know. Maybe… Maybe I should have… yes… hmm, none taken."

A week had passed since the wedding but whether or not Rohan's family was okay with what happened, they were all soon to find out.

"All right, bye uncle." Jatin hung up the phone

Geetha and her mother-in-law looked intently at him as he stared at the fan's reflection from his father's photo on the wall. The three of them were sitting in their living room on a bright Sunday morning.

"Well? Are you waiting for us to ask you?" Jatin's mother asked

"That was Rohan's uncle calling to ask what exactly happened at the wedding. Everyone was busy on that day, which is why he only noticed until it was too late when the argument had erupted between me and that weird old man."

Geetha and her mother-in-law continued to look intently at Rohan for the outcome of the call. Was a resolution made or would they never be invited to weddings again? On one hand, Geetha felt disappointed but on the other hand, she hated attention. Not being invited to weddings ever again was not a bad idea.

"I explained what had happened. Uncle agreed with me that the man was rude. It seems he was from the girl's side; one of their cousin's uncles."

"Okay, good, so the call went well." Asked Jatin's mother, "We don't have to worry."

"Not entirely, Ma." Jatin added, "Rohan's father agreed with me, I would say by 40%. The rest of his words seemed like 60% taunts."

Geetha's eyes widened but she didn't say a word. Her heart had already started sinking as she heard the words 60% taunts.

"How dare he taunt us? That old haggard broke the line and no one was saying anything. He was lucky you didn't break his skull for the things he was saying to you." Jatin's mother was infuriated.

"Yes, well... Rohan's father didn't care about that! He just interrupted me when I was trying to explain the events to him. His words sounded like he agreed but his tone was going in the opposite direction for a while until he finally said certain things. Then I realised that there is no point in saying or explaining anything because they have already judged us."

Geetha recalled how the old man broke the line and caused others behind him to follow him.

“What do you mean?” His mother asked, “What else did he say?”

“He said that it is okay, things happen. Can’t help it, especially, when you are not often invited to Lavish weddings. So, I first thought he said this for that old man but then he tells me not to take offence.”

There it was, that phrase again ‘high-society weddings.’ Geetha thought to herself.

“Does he mean we are not high-society people?” Geetha asked

“So, what are they trying to say? That we should not have stopped that man? Just let people break the line as they please. Is that how people behave in so-called *luxurious weddings*? Fine, next time, don’t invite us to such *high-society weddings*. Don’t bother going to their daughter’s wedding if they send an invitation.”

The word *high-society* kept haunting Geetha.

“*If*… they invite us, Ma.” Jatin looks at his mother, “It’s okay. The matter is over. So, we will also move on, which was something I did the moment we left from there. There is no point in dwelling on such things. What’s done is done.”

Geetha pondered to herself as her morning tea ran out of steam. If an elite wedding costs this much, then what would a middle-class society wedding cost? Saakshi is 7 and Diya is 4 years old; many years to go until they get married but… what would be the cost then?” She wondered whether her questions would remain without answers. She was hardly involved in the family’s decisions when it came to expenses. Did they have enough, or did they not have enough? It was a question that always left her at the receiving end of no response.

PART 2

"What is a megacity?"

Geetha held her breath for a response. The whiteboard awaited her next set of words after she wrote – Megacities. The students in the back row mumbled in soft interrupted tones, enough to make heads turn for the wrong reasons.

"Anyone… mega… cities?"

It was a sleepy day for a classroom full of yawning students, or maybe they were just that way with Geetha, is what she thought. The other lectures must not be as dull and sleep-induced.

Students in the front row stared at her like the people waiting helplessly in a cinema hall for a boring movie to end. Were they staring at the huge mole on her right cheek? Or, maybe they noticed how her saree looked tighter at the waist. Are you planning on getting heavier at the age of 32 already? Maybe that's what they were thinking about her. It could be why they were so distracted and not answering her question.

Snapping out of her disruptive thoughts, she desperately shoved aside the insecurities for a while, at least until the university bell rang.

Geetha stared back, wondering why she always hoped for an answer. In no classroom had she ever witnessed an answer floating her way. Out of the compulsion for the lecture to go on, a hand appeared in the ocean of 67 heads.

"Yes?" Geetha's prayers were answered

"Ma'am, a megacity is a large urban city."

While the student waited for her professor to approve of the answer, a sigh of relief appeared on Geetha's stoic expression, "Yes, to add to what you said, a megacity is an enormous city with a population exceeding 10 million people. Some examples can be Mumbai, Delhi, and Bangalore."

Students in the last row continued to talk. An annoyed student from the middle row looked back at them angrily but to no effect, they mumbled away. Geetha hesitated to stop them. What would she say? Stop talking...? Would they stop? Why would they stop?

Dejected by her thoughts that never ruled in her favour, she continued the lecture… "So, a megacity has different people which means that the cultures are also diverse. It has a more vibrant and dynamic atmosphere, unlike cities with a far smaller population. Such cities have different classes of people from low to…" There it was again, "high societies…" Would it ever leave her, she wondered.

"…But some unavoidable challenges are always part of huge cities such as…"

The lecture spiralled away into more yawns and deathly stares when it finally ended two hours later.

Placing her purse and book on the table, she takes out a bottle of water, drinks three sips, and gives a custom-made deathly stare at the wall clock. Just 10 more minutes to 5 pm and the day will grind to a halt.

"Tough day, today?" Professor Raghuram gives her a wide smile. His grey eyes shined behind a pair of high-powered spectacles.

"You know how it gets. One moment I am asking a question, and at another, the students have a question mark on their faces."

"Students will always be distracted. We're not meant to control how they respond, just teach and do the best you can."

"Hmm…" Geetha reluctantly agreed

"What's troubling you? You are usually not this vocal about your problems. It's not very often that you say more than one line in a conversation." Raghuram starts laughing.

Geetha wondered whether or not to disclose what she was feeling. She almost spoke up but stopped herself.

"Oh, spit it out already!" The professor said

"My husband fought at a relative's wedding. Someone tried to break into the meet-and-greet line. He was an old man. It had turned into a huge argument…"

Raghuram listened closely as Geetha laid out the facts and her observations. From the events that unfolded at the wedding to the phone call between Jatin and Rohan's father, she narrated all the facts.

"Hmm… so that's what's been troubling you."

"But something else was bothering me." Geetha opened up, "I heard that the wedding cost 42 Lakhs, give or take."

"Some cost even more." Raghuram pointed out

"If weddings can cost so much these days then what about when my daughters grow up and have to get married?"

Just then the University bell rang. It was time for everyone to leave. Geetha looked at the clock and placed her hand on her purse.

"Remove your hand from your purse." Professor Raghuram asks Geetha to stay back for a minute, "Wait for some time. Do you remember Professor Deboo? He retired six years ago. Actually, you had just joined at that time."

"That Parsi professor? I had met him briefly during the farewell get-together. Yes, I remember."

"Did you know that he had two more years to retire but he decided to leave earlier? He now also owns a 2BHK in Mahabaleshwar that costs around 1.5 Cr."

"Really? But as far as I know, we professors don't earn in crores."

"Well, he must have done something right. All those years he worked, he saved and invested money but how and what he did exactly is a conversation between you and him." Professor Raghuram took his mobile from his shirt pocket and made a few clicks. "I have sent you his number on WhatsApp. Give him a call."

PART 3

"But, why can't we just find out? Just to know a little more." Geetha sits on the bed, turning her head from left to right as her eyes follow Jatin's speed.

"It's too soon, Geetha." Jatin paces back and forth in their bedroom, walking with a pedometer on his foot, "They're still children and you are already planning on how to get rid of my daughters. They don't have to get married so soon."

"That is not what I meant. Wait… your daughters?"

"Okay, our daughters, of course." still pacing from the window to the room door, "What brought this upon you all of a sudden? And why are you worried about how much we will be able to spend on their wedding day? I already earn a decent salary. There's no need to worry."

Completing nearly 5000 steps, Jatin sits on the bed, panting and breaking a sweat. His back faced Geetha. "There's still time, you don't have to overthink so much."

Remorsefully looking out the window, Geetha watches a crow sitting in a tree outside their house. The crow incessantly fed her chicks, regurgitating food and then feeding it to them.. Oddly envious of the crow, Geetha observed how it had no money but was still capable of feeding her chicks.

"Yesterday, in the evening, I met Mrs. Joshi in the elevator. She asked me how I was doing. As usual, she had something to say about my waistline. I kept quiet, looking at her and then turning away. I waited patiently for the elevator to reach the ground floor. It was the regular Friday market day where the vegetables are lower priced compared to the other days. So, I assumed that just a few more floors and I will be out of this awkward conversation. But that lady went ahead and commented on *our* daughters."

Jatin turned his head, worried about what he was about to hear.

"She said that even though Saakshi has the same mole I have on my right cheek, she is sure someone good will come along in her life. Then she went further and said that Diya at least has her father's looks so she has a better chance of finding someone."

"I will talk to Mrs Joshi and give her a piece of my mind. She thinks she can say anything."

"Don't worry, this time, the words I could not utter from the 14th till the 3rd floor, I said it all from the 2nd to the ground floor until I walked away and went to the market. I think Mrs Joshi won't trouble us for a while."

"Wow, Geetha. You used words. My wife, who hardly speaks to people. Forget speaking, you don't even look in anyone's direction. What did you say? Mrs Joshi must have been dumbfounded."

"Yes, she was still wondering why I was angry. It's odd that some people don't realise how offensive they can be. I warned her never to compare my looks or the way our children look with anyone. I also told her that she doesn't need to worry about their future and that their parents can look after them."

"You used so many words. She must have been wondering whether it was Geetha she was talking to."

Jatin realised that Mrs Joshi was not talking to Geetha, the neighbour - but Geetha, the mother.

She got up and sat next to Jatin, placing her hand on his, "I am not trying to get rid of our daughters. I just want to make sure that their future is secure. All these years, I have never asked you how much money you saved or how we are doing financially. But this is important for our daughters. We go out for dinners every weekend just to give them a good time. We buy expensive gifts for their birthdays and new clothes during festivals so that they don't feel deprived. We also go on vacations during their school holidays to different places around India. If we can spend so much on these occasions then all I want to know is whether we are prepared for their wedding day. Not just for their wedding day but for their education, a secure future, retirement, including ours. All I am asking is that we just talk to an expert, someone who can guide us now so that we know how to handle the future."

> Has there ever been a moment of realisation that struck you during a conflict with someone? So much so, that it was enough to wake you up to reality, and feel just the way Geeta felt?
>
> It could have been your gut feeling, strong intuition, or even your logic calling out to you. Share and feel good to encourage others to scan this QR Code now.

Jatin sighed for a moment, "Okay since this means a lot to you, I will think of something. Of course, this is important for our daughters." Jatin stayed silent for a moment, allowing his thoughts to tell him what to do next, "I will ask the accountant where I work if he knows anyone we can talk to."

"I have already booked an appointment this Saturday with a finance consultant."

"When did you book? You didn't tell me!" Jatin stayed silent another moment, "Oh, so this conversation was just a way to convince me. And you didn't even discuss it with me before booking an appointment."

"I don't know a lot of things, Jatin, which is why I need you to come along with me. I had to take certain steps before discussing anything with you. I was afraid you would just brush it off. Any time, I would ask you about the family assets or the expenses you made for us, you would tell me to leave all of those worries to you. Ever since I was married to you, I was told to leave all money matters to you. I respect that but I am worried for our daughters. Don't I have a right to be involved?"

"So, you want me to involve you? Is that what this is all about?"

"Yes, of course! This is about our daughters and their futures. Do this for me just once."

Jatin took another deep breath of silence. Looking at Geetha, he rolled his eyes and then reluctantly said, "Okay… let's see what happens. I am doing this so you stop complaining about not being involved. You used to talk less; it was better that time…"

Jatin and Geetha waited at the reception. They arrived on time for the 11.00 am appointment. Seated in the front row, they looked around the waiting area where two more people were seated in the back row. Geetha fiddled with her fingers, memorising for the tenth time the questions she would ask or remind Jatin to ask in case she felt the urge to not speak, which was always the case.

Mr Hari's office looked professional. It was a silent commercial space where only enough was spoken in the background while phones rang for appointments.

"Mrs Geetha Shah? You can go in now. Take the first left and enter the first cabin."

Jatin and Geetha stood up and walked toward Mr Hari's cabin. His cabin was the first of the adjoining four cabins bridged in the same row across the hallway.

Jatin read the name written on the cabin door – Mr Hari Shastri, Financial Consultant, CFP, CFA, PFS. Already struck as a learned and professional expert, Jatin cautiously opened the cabin and allowed Geetha to enter first.

Mr Hari stood behind his Mahogany desk. When his eyes met theirs, he paused halfway before offering them chairs to sit.

The three most unanticipated people stood in one room, reluctantly letting go of the previous thought that they would never meet again. How wrong they were…

"So…" Mr Hari made the first attempt, "we meet again."

"Yes," Jatin said with a dry mouth, "I never thought we would."

Geetha started fiddling with her fingers again, waiting for Jatin to say something. They still didn't take their seats while Mr Hari also struggled to look at them.

"Please" the finance consultant finally gestured, "Have a seat."

The couple sat and gave a short glance at each other. Jatin noticed how Geetha's eyes flushed as she looked down at the floor. It would probably be the only direction into which she would look until the meeting was over.

"It was uhhh…" Mr Hari tried again, "quite an eventful wedding." The old man breathed heavily in his two-piece suit as he looked at Jatin.

"I guess, we were both… wrong in our own ways." Jatin extended the proverbial olive branch.

"Well, things happen." A gentle calm before the second storm, "I was right though. I mean it was not possible to go to the back of the line. Surely, you could have understood this because of my age. But anyway… all is in the past. I am sure we can move on."

Jatin waited for the next line where Mr Hari would have said that he was right too.

"You were right? Okay… you are older which justifies your point but…" Jatin looks at Geetha, who is still looking at the floor. "I was not wrong to request you to stand in the line where it started and not in the middle."

"Request? It was more like a threat."

Geetha squeezed Jatin's hand under the table, a silent plea for him to stand down. This wasn't the way their booked appointment was supposed to go, Jatin seemed to get the message.

"Look, Mr Hari," Jatin said, his voice calmer now, "I apologise for the outburst. I do regret whatever happened that day and I really wish I could undo everything. Unfortunately, I can't but the best thing I can do is offer my apologies."

"Thank you." The consultant replied gently and admitted a subtle wave of understanding, "Okay, I suppose, there is no way of looking at it only from my perspective. Fine, please go on."

"Thank you so much, Mr Hari." Jatin looks back at Geetha, takes a deep breath and then starts the conversation again, "Geetha, my wife," Jatin gestured the consultant toward Geetha, "spoke to Professor Deboo who used to work at the university where she works now as a professor. We believe he was your client. She reached out to him regarding the savings he built for years and the professor was kind enough to share your office number so we could meet you."

"Yes, he was my client. I still consult him on and off or just to ask how he is doing."

"Yes. So, that's why we're here because we're worried about our daughter's future. We want to make sure they have a good education and a secure future, and frankly, we don't know where to begin."

Geetha finally spoke up, "We heard about investment plans and budgeting, but it all seems so complicated."

Mr Hari's demeanour softened. He leaned back in his chair, a thoughtful look in his eyes. "It can seem overwhelming at first," he admitted, "but that's why I am here. Let's talk about your income, your current expenses, and your goals for your daughters. We can build a financial plan that fits your needs and gives you peace of mind."

Relief washed over Geetha. This was what she had hoped for all along – a sort of a visual map that showed them the way.

"Yes, I earn 8 lakhs a year. We have yet to calculate how much we spend every month. But regarding our goals, we want to make sure that our daughters are secured for their future, including their wedding day. It is the wedding expenses that we are worried about."

The next hour flew by as Mr Hari explained different investment options *"Think of your money as tree roots, "Mr. Hari said, sketching on a napkin. "FDs are the deep taproot—safe, but slow. Mutual funds?" He drew spreading branches. "They need storms to grow stronger. And this— "he circled the trunk," —is your emergency fund. No one admires roots, but they're what keeps the tree standing when the wind blows."*

Geetha traced the diagram. For the first time, the future felt less like a storm and more like something she could plant.

"It wouldn't be easy. There would be some adjustments but in the long run, you would be happier than any other family who has not done future planning for their children."

By the end of the consultation, they had a roadmap for their financial future. On their way out, Jatin smiled at Geetha.

Over the next few months, Jatin involved Geetha into the planning process. They started noting down every asset they had, from Jatin's and Geetha's yearly income to creating an opportunity of putting an apartment on rent.

Clubbing Jatin's 8 lakh and Geetha's 7.2 lakh annual income, they decided to save aside a specific portion to a joint fixed account, and two fixed deposits. The joint account was for their retirement, while the two fixed deposits were meant for their daughters.

To make sure they didn't just depend on the fixed deposits, they thought of other ways.

"Remember the bungalow my parents still live in?" Geetha asked Jatin

"Why don't we plan on living there after retirement? It's away from the city. It is still well maintained by my parents. Even though it is away from the city, the transport system has improved there so there is no problem or lack of access toward the city for anything."

"Yes, we have been to your parent's home several times. I would find it very peaceful there. Also, the city has a good hospital and medical clinics which we would need more of as we age."

"Well, I hope we will be healthy enough and not depend on medical assistance but rather have more of those long garden walks and fresh air." Geetha pointed out. "This way, we can save our retirement money on buying a new house. Rather we can move there and sublet this home once our daughters get married."

"This beautiful house on rent? No one deserves such an amazing house. They should pay us nothing less than 30k to 40k for rent."

"Yes, it is a beautiful house and that is why I am telling you it will fetch us a continuous flow of income during our retirement days."

"These days, I find it very hard to disagree with you." Jatin said

"Oh, in eight months, there has been quite a lot of progress. Very good." Mr Hari looked at the list of savings Jatin and Geetha were doing on a continuous basis.

	JATIN	**GEETHA**
Yearly income	8,00,000	7,20,000
Monthly (in-hand)	48,666	42,000
Home Expenses (monthly)	25,000	-
Miscellaneous · **Rent** · **Car maintenance/petrol** · **Bills (light, phone, etc.)**	23,000	-

Balance	666	42,000
Joint Account (monthly)	666	22,000
Fixed Deposit for Sakshi (yearly)	-	10,000
Fixed Deposit for Diya (yearly)	-	10,000

"By the end of ten years, you could potentially build a corpus of at least 4 crores." said Mr Hari

Jatin and Geetha were happy to hear more of what Mr Hari had to say. At least they knew they were headed in the right direction. "But we need to make a few changes from what I see." Mr Hari pointed out.

A look of worry settled on their eyebrows. They believed they had made the right calculations. "What I see now is that Geetha, you have Rs 22,000 in your account at the end of the month which you are contributing to your and Jatin's joint account. He is not able to contribute much because you both probably wanted to divide the expenses accordingly. I see that he is contributing more for the household expenses and for the bills. And you are contributing towards long term savings."

"Is that a problem?" Jatin asks, looking concerned.

"It might be in the long run." Mr Hari shows them the calculations on his laptop and compares it to their sheet of expenses. "So, you can reduce your home expenses, phone, and petrol bills. The other bills like your home rent or car insurance, light bill, and all these other expenses are unavoidable. So, keeping those aside, let us reduce your expenses slowly, starting from 2500 to 5000 a month." He shows them the calculation visually and revisits their spending approach, including investments.

STRUCTURE OF THE MONTHLY / YEARLY EXPENSES	JATIN	GEETHA
Yearly income	8,00,000	7,20,000
Monthly (in-hand)	48,666	42,000
Home Expenses (monthly)	20000	-
Miscellaneous · **Rent** · **Car maintenance/petrol** · **Bills (light, phone, etc.)**	20500	3000
Balance	8,166	39,000
Joint Account (monthly)	4,000	11,000
Fixed Deposit for Sakshi (yearly)	-	10,000 (one-time payment)
Fixed Deposit for Diya (yearly)	-	10,000 (one-time payment)
Remaining Balance	4,166	28,000

"You can also divide the unavoidable payments between each other. For instance, Geetha can pay the monthly rent so that lifts some burden off of you, Jatin. This way, you both still have some money left with you by the end of the month which you might probably use or not, depending on you."

But I just want to know whether you both have thought about creating a high-yield account for emergencies."

"We don't know how to do that," said Jatin.

"An emergency funds account is important because otherwise in the event something unforeseen happens, you will end up breaking an account that you used for your daughters or yourselves. Do one thing, apply for medical insurance for your family entirely and also add a small sum for now to a high-yielding account."

"We are not sure whether we can do that." Geetha says

"It is simple. From what I see, you both are still saving close to 4.27 Lakhs in a year. You don't have to use all but you can look at some good family packages. For instance, you can look to apply for a medical insurance of Rs 25000 and term insurance with premium of Rs 50,000 (a sum assured of 1 Crore) add one lakh to your emergency account. After this, you still have 1.27 lakh rupees left safe in your accounts, which now can be redirected partly to mutual funds

"I am worried because I also pay one lakh for my parents' medical insurance." Jatin points out.

"Okay, don't worry, you can keep growing money through your fixed deposits/mutual funds and circulate your money in the future." Said Mr Hari, "Let the money grow and I am there with you to see the progress."

Jatin and Geetha didn't realise this fine point but a wave of relief swept over them.

Have you recently calculated your monthly expenses? How about you start now…? Remember, you can add more columns just Geetha's was added next to Jatin's column of expenses.

You can categorise each type of investment for a goal

STRUCTURE OF MONTHLY/YEARLY EXPENSES (Your first step towards strategic financial planning)	**Your Column**	**Additional Column (if needed) of another earning member in the family**
Yearly income		
Monthly (in-hand)		
Home Expenses (monthly)		
Miscellaneous · **Rent** · **Car maintenance/petrol** · **Bills (light, phone, etc.)** • **Mediclaim / term insurance** • **Medical for parents etc**		
Balance		

Joint Account (monthly) - if applicable (retirement)		
Fixed Deposit/RD for ______ (yearly) (Education)		
Fixed Deposit for ______ (yearly) (Higher EDucation)		
in mutual funds (Marriage)		
Balance (Vacation etc , could be a short term goal)		

PART 4

Ten years flew by in a whirlwind of school plays, parent-teaching meetings, and birthday parties. Geetha and Jatin religiously followed the financial plan laid out by Mr Hari. They diligently contributed to their daughter's college funds, opting for a balanced mix of low-risk growth investments.

Low risk growth investments are financial instruments that offer a relatively low risk of capital loss while providing potential for moderate growth over time. These investments typically prioritise capital preservation and stability over high returns.

The different types of low risk growth investments:

- **Public Provident Fund (PPF):** A government-backed scheme with tax benefits and guaranteed returns.
- **Fixed Deposits (FDs & Recurring Deposits):** Offered by banks and offer fixed returns over a set period.
- **Hybrid Funds:** Hybrid funds are a type of mutual fund that invests in a mix of equity and debt securities. This diversification strategy aims to balance the potential for higher returns from equities with the relative stability of debt investments.
- **Small-Cap Funds:** Small-cap funds are mutual funds that invest in stocks of small-cap companies. These are companies with a relatively small market capitalization, typically less than ₹5000 crores. They offer higher growth potential with long-term wealth creation.
- **Gold:** Considered a safe haven investment, offering diversification and potential long-term appreciation.

Every month they reviewed their budget, making adjustments for their growing household expenses. There were tough choices – nights spent debating between buying a new television or prioritising an additional contribution to their investment. But at each step of adhering to their plan, their resolve grew stronger.

One evening, as Geetha helped their elder daughter, Sakshi , with her college applications, a familiar sense of accomplishment washed over her. Sakshi, a bright young girl, had received acceptance letters from several prestigious universities. They discussed the financial aid packages, their eyes scanning the scholarship amounts and loan options.

"Remember how scared we were ten years ago?" Geetha asked with a hint of amusement in her voice.

Sakshi chuckled. "Actually, no. But I do remember all those times you told me about the importance of saving."

Jatin walked in with a plate of sliced fruits. "We're still not out of the woods yet" he said, placing the plate on the table.

Sakshi, ever the pragmatist, pointed out, "But Dad, there were times when it felt like we were depriving ourselves. When will that end?"

"Were we?" Jatin felt a sinking feeling in his gut when his daughter pointed out the times they had to say no to buying certain items for their children.

"Of course, remember that lovely gown I wanted to buy for my friend's wedding. You and mom instead got one stitched. I mean it was nice but I wanted that gown."

Geetha smiled at Sakshi, "Beta, that dress cost ten times the amount of what we got for you. Accha tell me, where else would you have worn that gown?"

"I don't know… maybe at some other wedding.. oh but then what if someone else noticed that it was the same gown I wore in the previous wedding."

"Now tell me," Geetha added another question, "this tailored dress that your father and I got for you. Have you worn it again?"

Sakshi thought for a while, "Not really. That's the only time I wore it."

"Hahahaha..." Jatin laughed, It was a real headache to think of these expenses and then compare prices. Oh the arguments your mother and I had sometimes about whether she can buy a new purse again and whether I can buy a Harley-Davidson for road trips."

"Which your father never took." Geetha pointed out

"Well, I would have taken such trips had I bought that bike. They still have it in the showroom."

"Maybe those days are not far !!!" Geetha rolled her eyes

Over the next few years, they saw both Sakshi and their younger daughter, Diya, graduate from college, debt-free and ready to embark on their careers.

Mr Hari had the front row seats to their daughter's weddings. This time, he didn't have to cut any lines. He was given first preference wherever he went, considering how he had aged and was chauffeured around in a wheelchair.

Sakshi and Diya's weddings were celebrated with a tinge of grandeur. Jatin and Geetha managed to raise two crore rupees for their daughters' weddings.

"Oh, you both still managed to spend so much on Sakshi and Diya's weddings?" Asked Mr Hari as he sat at a table at Diya's wedding.

"Well, actually, we have spent much less. Sakshi's wedding cost about 80 lakhs and Diya's wedding was around the same amount."

"Oh, what happens to the rest of the amount?" Mr Hari asked curiously

"We have split the balance between Sakshi and Diya so they can add the amount to their savings." Geetha said

"That is good thinking." Mr Hari smiled, "Well, I will head home now. Thank you for inviting me. The food was great."

Mr Hari left the wedding. The celebrations had gone well. Jatin and Geetha bid farewell to Diya and her husband. A bittersweet moment of all the years gone by. Geetha handed a tissue to Jatin as he cried while watching his daughter leave in a car that had a board on the back written - just married.

The celebrations settled down with a soft silence in the air. The night had ended on a sweet note. Sakshi spent the night at her parent's house. The next morning, she woke up to her parent's hurried footsteps.

"What is up with the both of you?"

"Did you forget again?" Geetha asked as she tied her shoe laces, "Your father and I are going for a road trip."

"That's today? I can barely keep my eyes open." said Sakshi

"I bought a Harley-Davidson. I am going to drive us around India for the next couple of months. It's going to be fun."

"Us? I am too tired."

"Oh not you, Sakshi. Your mother and I are going. Keep up."

Still yawning, she squints with sleepiness in her eyes. Her parents wearing leather jackets in their 50s was a rare sight she thought she'd never see."

"Come quick!" Jatin shouted out at Sakshi, extending his smartphone to her.

She walks wobbly in her sleep, takes the smartphone, knowing just what was expected. Click, click, click!

"Thanks Sakshi. I will send these to the family group so Diya can also see them."

"I'm going back to sleep." Sakshi walks back into the house hearing the deep-throated throttle of their bike fading into the distance.

Jatin and Geetha, initially overwhelmed by the prospect of their daughters' future financial needs, sought guidance from a financial consultant, Mr. Hari. Together, they developed a comprehensive financial plan:

Key Strategies:

1. **Budgeting:**
   - They meticulously tracked their income and expenses.
   - They identified areas for potential savings, such as reducing household expenses.
   - They allocated specific amounts for essential needs, discretionary spending, and savings and focusing on their goals
2. **Emergency Fund:**
   - They established an emergency fund to cover unexpected expenses.
   - They prioritised medical insurance for their family.
3. **Retirement Planning:**
   - They set aside a portion of their income for retirement savings.
   - They considered the potential of renting out their current home after retirement.
4. **Children's Education and Marriage:**
   - They created dedicated savings accounts for their daughters' education and marriage.
   - They explored low-risk growth investments like fixed deposits and mutual funds.

5. Long-Term Success:

By consistently adhering to their financial plan, Jatin and Geetha were able to:

- Secure their daughters' future education and marriage.
- Build a comfortable retirement fund.
- Achieve financial independence and peace of mind.

Their journey highlights the importance of early financial planning, disciplined saving, and seeking expert advice.

One-Minute Financial Hack!!!

Feeling overwhelmed by finances? **Allocate** your income to needs, wants, and savings. Then, **automate** transfers to dedicated savings accounts right after payday. This simple hack builds financial security effortlessly.

Book Club Chats
• If you were Jatin and Geetha, what steps would you take to save on your monthly expenses? • Do you think opening so many savings or long-term investment accounts were justified for Jatin and Geetha? • Was there any other investment they could have made in place of fixed deposits?

Potential Roadblocks: How to Handle

1. Unexpected Large Expenses

- **Hindrance:** A sudden, major expense (e.g., medical emergency not fully covered by insurance, home repair).
- **Resolution:** Consistently build and maintain a robust **emergency fund** in a high-yield account, ensuring immediate access to liquid cash.

2. Investment Underperformance

- **Hindrance:** Low-risk growth investments (like FDs or some hybrid funds) might not grow as expected, impacting long-term goals.
- **Resolution:** Regularly **review and diversify** investments with a financial advisor, adjusting the portfolio to balance risk and growth potential.

3. Lifestyle Creep/Sacrifice Fatigue

- **Hindrance:** Increasing desire for discretionary spending as income grows, or feeling deprived from current sacrifices.
- **Resolution:** Periodically **revisit their budget** and celebrate small financial milestones to stay motivated, allowing for controlled discretionary spending as goals are met.

Rathandeep's Kaleidoscope

Your financial journey doesn't have to be complicated. Start by clearly defining your goals and seeking expert guidance. With **disciplined budgeting**, consistent **saving**, and smart **investing**, you can build a secure future, just like Jatin and Geetha. The peace of mind is truly priceless.

Back in the garden

"Wow, so where did you travel to on your Harley-Davidson?" Bhavani asked Geetha.

"Oh, we went to a lot of places, starting from our city, we headed up north to Goa, then to Punjab, and from there we moved across the north and the east. At times, it was tiring so we went back home and took a month's break. But Jatin and I had a lot of fun, we met a lot of people, and made so many friends. Then we pushed off again, this time with a better understanding of how our GPS system worked."

"I guess that was all possible because of the savings you'll had done." said Shivani

"Yes, it was indeed. I wish we could have gone when we were younger, like maybe in our 30s or 40s, but that's when we were busy building our savings."

"Plus, where would you leave Sakshi and Diya while you went on your second honeymoon on a Harley-Davidson?" Meetha said, laughing and winking at Geetha.

They all laughed while taking their second round of drinks and snacks. "Okay, so before we wrap up this evening, let's do one more story this evening. Then we can come back here next week." Geetha said

"That's a good idea." said Bhavani, "Who do we pick next?"

They looked around at each other, "Meetha, why don't you end this evening with your experience?" Shivani said

"Me? Okay, why not!" Meetha paused for a while and then began, "My story begins when my son had a seizure and it had been a long time since he had one. But the reason behind his attack was where it all started..."

A FAMILY RIFT, A SON WITH SPECIAL NEEDS, & A FUTURE UNKNOWN

PART 1

182 days. That's how long it had been since Sanju's last seizure. Meetha held her breath, counting each ragged gasp her ten-year-old son expelled. Her husband, Lalit, wrestled the blankets free, their faces etched with worried lines. Sweat beaded on Meetha's forehead as Sanju's body contorted.

Meetha had to wrestle Sanju as he was thrust out of his sleep with the tremors that raged through his body. A while later, the tremors left the boy limp and bewildered in Meetha's arms. His eyes, vacant for a moment, spiralled him back into exhaustion.

In the sterile silence of the moment, the diary on the bedside table mocked her with its stark entry from six months ago. Today, a new description, time, and day would scar its pages, a grave reminder of the shattered normalcy.

A few moments later, Sanju returned to regular breathing and was relieved of the seizure. Meetha was reminded of the other side of her reality. They were leaving. Today was the day. The weight of their decision, heavy and unspoken, hung thick in the air, a burden that claimed Lalit's and Meetha's sleepless nights, even weighing young Sanju's limp body.

"You go and count the bags," Lalit told Meetha, "I will look after Sanju."

Meetha gently passes Sanju towards Lalit, shoulders herself up from the bed, and walks out of the bedroom, worry lines permanently stuck to her face.

Sanju was barely 2 when his parents noticed how he rarely made eye contact, retreated into his own silent world, and lined up his toy cars with an almost ritualistic precision. When the doctors diagnosed him with Autism Spectrum Disorder, Meetha and Lalit felt like they were punched in the gut.

Eight years passed since the seizures trampled their way into their son's life. Meetha checks the bags in the living room as Nirmal, her brother-in-law, sits in his room. His wife, Mira, stands in the living room, hesitant to offer any help. "Meetha, should I…"

"It's okay, bhabhi." Meetha stops her in her tracks, noticing Mira walking towards her to help her lift the bags to the van outside. "We will manage."

Their home—once alive with the chaos of nine voices, the clatter of shared meals, the warmth of generations under one roof—now stood hollow. Only four remained, their footsteps echoing like ghosts in the empty halls. Meetha looked around the house, probably the last day she, Lalit, and their son, Sanju were to ever step foot once they left.

Mira runs into the kitchen while Meetha is still checking to account for every bag and suitcase. She turns around to go into the room to find Lalit bringing Sanju out while he is still asleep, tired from the seizure attack. "I will place him in the car and tell the movers to put our luggage in the van."

Meetha sees Lalit carry Sanju out, watching her husband's overall posture decline further as their problems age. Never did she imagine this day would come, and yet, here they were.

She notices Mira rushing out from the kitchen and running towards her, "Please don't say no to this," placing a plastic container sealed with a tight cover in Meetha's hands. "It will be a long journey, and Theplas are your favourite, isn't it Meetha? Even Sanju likes to have them. Please, don't say no." Meetha helplessly shivers a smile beneath her drooping cheeks. A flashback of how the family would sit together to enjoy hot Theplas with sweet tamarind chutney and masala tea. A time when laughter and silly jokes would travel around every corner of their home. Now, the memorable snack exchanged between the two sisters-in-law lacked the sweetness of the tamarind sauce. Mira was always the one to make the Theplas while Meetha made the Tamarind sauce. Now that she was leaving, sweetness resigned halfway.

It all began 18 months after the passing of Meetha's in-laws when Nirmal, Lalit's elder brother wanted to rent a part of the house.

"Don't be an emotional fool. It's been more than a year since Ma and Baba have passed away. So, what if we rent their room to someone else? It's not a big deal. Everyone does it."

"Who does this, Nirmal?" Lalit retorts with a question, agitated by the thought of renting their parent's room to strangers, "We are not a B&B company. We won't just give a room on rent to someone. Who is going to look after their needs? And renting our parent's room! Who has given you this idea?"

The wives look on as Lalit and Nirmal lock horns with each other. Mira sends her children to their room. Meetha sits with Sanju on the sofa opposite the television showing cartoons on low volume.

"Think objectively, Lalit. Expenses are increasing. You don't see an increment happening at your job any time soon. My boss has already given an advance that we used for Ma and Baba's medical treatments. We have to pay that back to my boss. How will we do that? By getting over-emotional about everything?"

"What about the second home Baba had bought years ago? Can we not put that house on rent? Their room in this house is not an option."

"That second home is in a location that will not fetch a good monthly rent. But here, we can get proportionally higher for just one room."

"I don't agree with this decision. I am telling you again, Nirmal, giving Ma and Baba's room on rent is not an option."

"Not an option…?" Nirmal mocks Lalit. He looks at Meetha. "Meetha! Looks like you didn't pour your husband strong tea today. He is talking in his sleep." Then looking back at Lalit, he says, "You can barely sustain your son's medical expenses, you don't even earn as much as I do. You think you can decide what is and what is not an option. Lalit, you have lost the right to decide that… from now on, after Baba, I am the decision-maker in this house. If you don't like it then either sit quiet or there is no place for you here."

Those were the last words Lalit took with him as he placed Sanju in the car. Meetha sat in the back with Sanju as he lay asleep. The last memory of a home that resonated with them now left a bitter taste. Meetha looked back, seeing Mira standing at the main door looking at Meetha. Tears flowed from her eyes but the deed was done and there was no looking back.

PART 2

"It had been six months since Sanju's last seizure. The frequency had reduced. Previously, the attacks would be paced two months apart. For a change, I started getting used to not seeing my son struggle in pain."

Everyone in the support group looked on at Meetha. It was her turn to speak among the parents encircled. "Last Friday was a sad day for Sanju. He sensed that he was never going to see his cousins again. I think the stress triggered his seizure and woke him up from his sleep. He still looks out the window, thinking his cousins will come to meet him."

The support group for parents was a biweekly affair. They would sit in a circle, each one being allowed to talk about their experience, struggles, and progress concerning their children who were on the autism spectrum. Raising a child with special needs would have been a challenge for any parent. Having a close-knit group that resonated with one's struggles offered respite to Meetha and Lalit.

Thirty minutes later, the group was done for the day. Each one talked about their experiences personally with one or two parents. Meetha and Lalit were taking some snacks from the table where sandwiches and other homemade food were often made and brought by some parents. Due to the packing and unpacking in the new home, Meetha couldn't find the time to make the regular spinach and corn cheese samosas that she would make.

"No samosas?" Avinash's voice dropped to a theatrical whisper. "Meetha, you've left us starving. My son's been asking since yesterday—'Papa, is today samosa day?'"

Meetha smiled, a little wave of happiness swept over her tired face, "Oh, I didn't realise it. We have been busy with shifting and managing things. We have moved to our second home."

"Oh, congratulations. Where have you shifted?"

Lalit felt like receiving more of a 'I am sorry to hear that' response. If only they knew why they had to shift. Maybe they should keep a support group for families experiencing rifts, he thought to himself.

They spoke a bit about the place they moved to and how it would now take an hour to reach these biweekly meetings. But they didn't mind as the environment at the support group seemed familiar, making Lalit and Meetha feel a kind of warmth and closeness to one another.

"No samosas?" A mother from the support group asked while approaching the table of snacks.

"They were busy. They just shifted to a new home." Said Avinash, standing next to them.

"Oh, that's too bad. I mean, congratulations. I am happy for you. Must be exciting." Said the mother, trying to cover up her dismay about the absence of her favourite snacks. "You know, I usually grab some of your samosas to go. My daughter, Alka, loves them. She doesn't mind me leaving her home with her grandparents as long as I bring back home these samosas." Coming closer to Meetha, she whispers, "Sometimes I come less for these meetings and more for your samosas."

Meetha grew a wider smile, unable to believe her ears. "That's very kind of you, Mrs Yagnik. I will bring more next time, and make extra, especially for Alka."

"Really? That would be great. She loves them."

"In that case, if you can please make some for me also, I will take some back with me." said the father

Lalit and Meetha looked at each other not realising how much her homemade samosas were appreciated.

*"Meetha," Mrs Yagnik leaned in, her eyes glinting. "Those samosas aren't just tasty—they're clever. The spinach for iron, the cheese for protein... You're still a Nutritionist at heart, aren't you?"*During one of our group sessions, I remember you saying that

you had to quit so you could give your son the care he needs. You are one still.

"Yes, that's true. We needed one of us to stay back for Sanju at home or while helping him at the special school for children. One thing that's good about these weekend group sessions is that they have a special centre for bringing our children while Lalit and I can attend these sessions."

"Well, what about now?" Mrs Yagnik was aware of the care centre for the children to be looked after but her concern was towards the samosas, "You should start selling these samosas. I don't mind paying you for them. They are really good. That way, I don't have to wait two weeks to eat them."

Lunchtime was quiet. Sanju was eating his food while he kept noticing the missing chairs at the table. Every time he looked around, his cousins were not in the house. The table felt smaller while his mother and father ate their food in silence. Meetha helped Sanju if he needed more to eat. She made his favourite vegetable.

Lalit looked at Meetha. She looked back at him, wondering about the glint of a smile on his face. "What happened?" She grew curious.

"You must miss working as a Nutritionist."

Meetha paused chewing her food for a moment while she looked on at Lalit. Where was his line of thought stemming from? She wondered if it was because of what happened at the support group this morning.

"You had to leave your job ten years ago because of..." Lalit paused, "You must be wondering what life could have been like." He paused again, "Do you?"

Meetha remembered all the times she sat at home on weekdays wondering how her clients were progressing with their diet programs. Whether her fellow nutritionists had anything new to talk about regarding their discoveries with eating behaviours and metabolic responses of different people. Her colleagues had kept in touch for the first two years after Sanju was born. After that, Meetha was always busy and she never realised when she drifted into Sanju's world completely, leaving everyone out of her life.

"I don't understand," bringing herself back to the dining table, "What made you think of this all of a sudden?"

"It's not like I never thought about how you must have felt. We both became so busy as parents and it never got easy. Almost every day, we had to learn so many new things about autism, and you, especially. At least, I could go to work. The abrupt pause in your career must not have been easy for you to experience."

Meetha smiled, realising that Lalit was contemplating something since their time at the support group today.

"It wasn't easy. That's true. I did miss my job as a Nutritionist. That is also true. But after a point of time, none of it mattered because there was hardly any time to miss it. Sanju was my priority, our priority."

"Would you want to start again? As a Nutritionist?"

"Oh..." Meetha thought for a while, "It's been ten years, Lalit. I have not updated myself in the field. I don't know if I can continue where I left off. Getting a job also would not be easy."

"What if you tried a part-time job? Sanju's school is in the morning till noon. What if you could work part-time somewhere?"

"I don't know, Lalit. That's a lot to think about. Now that we have moved to this house, a lot of places are far from us. Be it the support group or his school, they are both always going to be an hour away."

"Hmm..." Lalit continued eating, "Maybe... I just thought that maybe you would want to get back to working."

"I do miss it sometimes but I am not sure whether it is the right time. I could probably think about it after a few years. I don't know,

Lalit." The more Meetha thought about it, the more she was confused, "Besides, who will give me a job after a 10-year gap?"

There was no denying that Meetha's career had taken a steep dip unless she revived it in some way or the other. Needless to say, Lalit's question kept her busy in thought for a few days, wondering whether getting back into the workforce would be good for her. For once, she too could help add to Lalit's earning capacity. However, so many questions cropped up as she went deeper into the thought of working again.

Who would look after the house? What if she had to leave work due to an emergency at school? What if she didn't get a part-time job that suited her schedule? What has changed in the world of nutrition?

The thought of re-entering the workforce seemed more daunting than when she entered fresh over ten years ago.

PART 3

A new week had begun. Lalit was back home from work. He enters the house, the weight of the day on his shoulders. He sees Meetha sitting on the sofa and sighs, kicking off his shoes with a thud. Sanju runs up to him, flapping his hands excitedly. Lalit manages a weak smile and pats Sanju's head.

Meetha looks at Lalit, her brow furrowed with concern. "How was work?" she asks.

Lalit hesitates, avoiding her gaze. "Not good," he mutters, collapsing onto the sofa next to Meetha. Sanju climbs onto the sofa between them, oblivious to the tension in the air.

Meetha places a hand on Lalit's arm. "What happened?"

Lalit takes a deep breath. "They are downsizing." He says, his voice tight, "The company."

Meetha's eyes widened. "What? Do you mean…?"

Lalit nods, his face grim, "They let me go."

Sanju looks up at his parents, sensing a change in the atmosphere. He whimpers and crawls off the sofa, retreating to a corner of the room. Meetha's anger subsides, replaced by a wave of despair. Sinking back into the sofa, she buries her face in her hands.

Lalit reaches out and touches her arm gently. "Meetha, we'll get through this. We always do."

Meetha doesn't respond. Tears well up in her eyes. She feels lost and scared. Again, she is bewildered by the questions that crowd her mind. How will they manage? What will the future hold for them; for their son?

Before Lalit could say anything else, Meetha walks into the kitchen. Lalit, perplexed with the situation, allowed the silence between them to take its course. Looking at Sanju playing with his toy, he wished life was somewhat simpler than what it was now.

This sudden turn of events kept Meetha awake at night. Her mind racing with thoughts. She looked at Lalit asleep and tired of the burdens he carried. Maybe it was time for her to take up a job but who would give her a job after ten years of not practising as a Nutritionist? Every possible worst-case scenario popped into her mind like a film snapshot unfolding before her eyes.

What would happen if they could not pay for Sanju's therapy? What about his school fees? What about the light bill? What if they have to go back to living with his brother? Maybe things would get better but what if it gets worse?

Maybe she should call her old colleagues to ask and see if there was an opening for her. Ten years have passed. She barely kept in touch. What would she say? Would they answer her call? Would they help? They could be busy in their lives, so helping her might be out of the question.

She felt her thoughts weighing heavy on her eyelids. Maybe it was time to call it a night. Stressing about it at night wouldn't get her anywhere. So, she realised that it was better to fall asleep. It must be midnight anyway or so she thought. She turned to look at the watch on her side table, it was 2.30 am.

"How are you, Meetha." Mira's voice brought a sense of familiarity and warmth the family once shared together.

"We have seen better days, bhabhi." Meetha said, judging the silence between them on the phone, "How are you?"

"I am fine." Mira almost welling up in her voice, "But the kids and I miss you and Sanju. They miss their uncle too. Nirmal doesn't say anything but I know he is missing his younger brother."

"Sometimes I think about it and I feel sad that it had to turn out this way."

"Yes, it makes me sad too." Said Mira. "How is Lalit's work?"

Meetha almost choked before she could say anything, "Yes, it's going on. Almost everything is an hour away. Sanju's school, the therapy centre, and of course, Lalit's workplace."

"I wish we were still all together. Having a big family at home. The laughter, the noise, and even the arguments, it all felt so lively. Now that you, Lalit and Sanju are not here, our home feels so... dead. I don't know how to deal with this environment at home. The air is just different even when we wake up in the morning."

"It is the same here. We call it our second home but it is nothing like how it used to be when we all lived together. I can't believe almost ten days have passed since we moved here but time goes by very slowly. We are still trying to settle in but it feels weird."

"What can you and I do? Both our husbands made this decision on their own and didn't even think how it would affect all of us."

Meetha couldn't agree more. It was just like how Lalit kept the news of losing his job from her for two months. "I think whatever we do, we must not sit on it and just think about it. **Action is required.** Every time, feeling helpless won't lead us anywhere."

"What do you mean, Meetha? Should I be talking to Nirmal and tell him to make peace with Lalit?"

Meetha felt like the words she spoke were more for her than for Mira. Her thoughts percolated into the family feud, making her unsure of how to respond.

"No, well… It's too early now. Maybe we should wait for a few months more."

"No, but Meetha, you are right. I have also been thinking. We can't just let the two brothers decide how they want to end this. We are a family. And it's not right that we allow this separation to carry on for too long."

"So bhabhi, are you thinking of talking to Nirmal?"

"Maybe, I mean, why not? He hasn't spoken about it since Lalit and you left."

The conversation went on as Meetha started to reflect on what she said, '*Action is required*'.

PART 4

Three days had passed. Lalit came home tired and worn out from the one-hour trip by train. Just a few more steps into the house and he would have hit the bed drifting into dreaming of a multiverse where everything was perfect.

But this time, maybe the multiverse had reached him first.

Today, Lalit came home to a completely different home. Tiffins spread across their dining table; foils wrapped around different foods. The aroma of spices filled up their space like the way it was back home with his brother. He felt a familiar atmosphere when Mira and Meetha would serve lunch on a Sunday afternoon and the whole family would sit together to enjoy their meals. A time even when the grandparents were alive and everyone was together, happy and united. Alas, the food remained but with fewer faces.

“Meetha?” For a moment, Lalit looked around, wondering whether he entered the wrong house by mistake.

Sanju comes running to hold his father. Lalit hugs Sanju, asking him where his mother was and a second later, Meetha walks out of the kitchen. Holding a tray of assorted snacks, she noticed Lalit standing next to the dining table holding Sanju’s hand.

“Oh, you’ve come. Give me some time, I will make some tea for you.”

She rushes back into the kitchen. Lalit follows her, “This kitchen has seen better days. What is happening? Meetha, are you going through some midlife crisis?”the

Meetha gives Lalit a confused look. “Midlife…? Lalit, I cooked all these dishes. I have an idea. I think, no… no more thinking. Action is required.”

“Action…? What are you talking about?” Lalit is confused. All he could see was Meetha rushing in and out of the kitchen, either switching off the gas stove or pouring the contents of one vessel into another.

“Okay, that’s the last one.”

Lalit follows Meetha into the living room. She places a dish on the table. All is laid in an organised manner from her famous cheese spinach samosas to Hazelnut biscuits, Ragda Patties, Vegetable Puffs, Mixed Vegetable and Paneer Pulav, Hara Bhara Kebabs, Potato Wedges, Jeera Rice, Makhani Dal, Theplas with Tamarind Chutney, and a few other dishes. Ahead of each plate or tray was a label neatly placed with the dish named on it. Taking out the phone from her pocket, she starts clicking photos.

“Meetha…? What are you doing?” A hint of worry in his voice, Lalit stands still wondering whether Meetha has invited the whole neighbourhood for a feast or she started a new Instagram account.

“Look at this…” Meetha takes out a sheet of paper from her bag and hands it over to Lalit. He starts reading the paper, an A-4 sheet that reads – "*Meetha's Homemade Food*" – showing an organised list of dishes from starters to main courses, appetisers, and desserts.

"I am going to sell food, less oil, less ghee, and more nutrients. Healthy food for everyone."

Lalit stands with the paper in his hands, "You will start what?"

"A food business from home. Home-cooked food. I even spoke to our support group host yesterday and they said they would not mind paying me a small sum to deliver homemade snacks to them every day. They have different sessions conducted daily and they need someone who can bring some good snacks."

Lalit was still taking in the news he just received, "When did this happen?"

"Three days ago, I had an idea. Mrs Yagnik and the others liked the cheese spinach samosas I made. I thought that since I love cooking food then why not start delivering home-cooked meals."

> Have you ever experienced a time in your life, where as a woman, you had to finally take matters into your own hands?
> Most women are conditioned to believe that the man of the house knows best. So, he knows what he is doing. Let him decide! He won't take his wife's advice, anyway…
> In all honesty, he is also a human, only human, and should not be carrying such a great responsibility of life's reroutes. It should be a responsibility of both the partners.
> So, let me know whether, as a woman, was there ever a time when you made a decision and did what you thought was best? Or, are you thinking that it is time for you to take action about something instead of waiting for someone else to do it for you?
> Scan this QR Code to let us know your action plan for a brighter future . It will help a lot more women like you know.

Meetha showed Lalit all the dishes she made. Sanju took a tour around the dining table, taking in the aroma of his mother's delicious food. Lalit could see the enthusiasm trickling all over his wife's face as she brimmed with excitement over her new idea. Just then he notices some dishes that he never saw Meetha ever make.

"I thought you didn't know how to make Theplas." Lalit took a piece of the vibrant green fleck of fenugreek leaves kneaded skilfully into the dough and dipped it in the Tamarind sauce. After taking a bite, "This tastes like…" and suddenly he realised, "Was Mira here?"

"Yes, Mira helped me make these Theplas, potato wedges, and those Hara Bhara kebabs over there." She points out to the edge of the table

"Why is Mira helping you? Did you tell her about my job?"

"We didn't have time to discuss anything about you."

"She left before I came home?"

"Yes, of course, otherwise she would have reached home after your brother came from work."

"Why didn't you tell me that you were cooking up these ideas in the kitchen with your sister-in-law?"

"I needed more clarity before I could tell you anything."

"Meetha, this is a decision we should be taking together."

"Oh? Now you want to make decisions together. When you and your brother decided to split our family in half, were any of us asked? Just got the bags packed and moved out. Sanju was also so stressed because of that!"

Sanju covered his eyes leaving a bit of visual room like he was about to get a jump scare from a horror movie. Lalit looked at Sanju realising that Meetha already knew how the conversation would go.

"Okay, okay. I thought about these things but you know how Nirmal can get. He is very stubborn and he kept waving his income status flag in my face. What was I supposed to do? And he told us to leave, it was not my decision alone."

"You are right! The both of you made this horrible decision without asking your wives about it." Meetha allowed Lalit to take a sigh of relief, immediately after which she continued, "So, that it's decided that you both were wrong, let me get back to what Mira Bhabhi and I have been planning. I was thinking about the food that Mira Bhabhi and I can make together and sell. She and I can cook a variety of dishes together. She said she is ready to help me."

"Nirmal will take credit for that also."

"Is that what you are worried about? Tell me, do you want to think about what your brother will think about you or how we will manage our livelihood if you don't get a job?"

"I will get a job."

"Good then, you will get a job, and I will have my business with Mira Bhabhi. You don't have to worry. Lalit, we have to also make sure to continue paying for the special care plan for Sanju. I feel we can do more. What about when we grow old? We have focused so much on our son's wellbeing, we have to also look out for ourselves when we get older, don't you think?"

At the back of his mind, Lalit knew that Meetha had a valid point. If she could start something of her own then it would help them create a budget, and track their income and expenses.

"All this is fine, Meetha, but this is all just sinking in my head now. I need some time to process everything."

"Okay. Take your time. I understand. But I will be going ahead with this plan. As it is, our support group has already given me a business to start with and it starts from Monday."

Lalit stands in an absolutely still position. Meetha recognised the look on his face. Lalit always stood still whenever he was in deep thought. She knew it was a good sign because it meant he was in agreement and he was thinking of the steps they could take ahead.

"So, how are you and Mira Bhabhi going to deliver the food? Also, how will people know you are selling homemade food?"

Meetha was a little confused, "I don't know yet. I just started it because I didn't want to waste any more time. Action is important. I will need to buy several food containers."

"Okay, so we will have to allot a budget for that plus we will have to think about marketing your business and getting more customers through some kind of sales strategy."

"Oh, I don't know any of these things. I was just thinking that you can tell your office people that your wife has started her own business and sells homemade, healthy food. See if they would be interested."

"And what if they are not interested? I can do that for sure but then we need to make sure we keep getting the orders. Marketing is a way to make sure that your business continues to run. We will also need to make sure that you have enough time to do all these things. You will need more sets of hands to help you grow your business. We will have to hire people and probably some food-making equipment too."

"So, what do we do?" Meetha started to get worried. "I didn't think so far ahead. Maybe you're right. Maybe this isn't such a good idea."

Lalit stood still again. Sanju went to pacify his mother as she sat on the sofa already regretting her decision. "What if I do a bad job? Everyone will think the worst of me. It will be so awkward at the support group. They'll look at me and say, *oh it's Meetha; the one whose business didn't pick up. Such a shame.* Oh no, this is a disaster."

"Calm down, Meetha. Do you remember Avinash Gujjar? He was praising your cheese spinach samosas at the support group session."

"Yes, but just because he was praising one snack item does not mean that I can do a good job."

"No, no, don't think about that... look, you are off to a good start. So, don't worry. I mentioned Avinash because he works in an online media and print marketing company. What if we can ask him to help us with your business?"

"Will he help us?"

"If he wants those cheese spinach samosas coming his way then why not? You leave the talking to me."

A few days later, Lalit and Meetha met with Avinash at the company where he works. They took up the lowest package deal to start with and see how they do with the sales and marketing approach.

Lalit got a new job after three months. He did not provide a significantly higher pay but he did manage to get a decent hike to a monthly pay of Rs 65,000 per month. Meanwhile, Meetha's homemade food business was gradually picking up with the support group.

The income she received for doing business with the support group was Rs 10,000 per month. She and Mira kept aside Rs 5,000 per month and the remaining Rs 5,000 they spent on food supplies. Lalit saved Rs 20,000 from his monthly salary in another account to make sure that they could opt for a better sales and marketing package plan as the initial package they took wasn't giving them customers that converted.

“If we want to make more money, we will have to spend more money but also make sure that the media company where Avinash works uses a better sales and marketing approach. These days online marketing works better. We will have to talk more about how your homemade food has less deep fried oily food and more nutritious ingredients.” Lalit told Meetha

“So far Mira bhabhi and I have managed to save Rs 15000 in three months. I don’t think it is enough. But you were about to save Rs 60,000 in three months. So, that leaves us with Rs 75,000. So, by next month, we should have 1 lakh rupees.” Meetha smiled at Lalit

“See, I told you. We will get there soon! See, their marketing and sales package is much more expensive than what we have saved so far. So, I will have a talk with Avinash about what can be done. Maybe we should hire a freelancer or a smaller business. They may charge us less. Plus, we have to also make sure we create some savings. Otherwise, we may end up spending whatever we have saved by now.”

“What if we learn a bit about marketing? There are so many blogs I read on interesting marketing tips. I also went through some YouTube videos. If we can apply some of those marketing tips, we could also get somewhere.” Meetha said

A few days had passed. It was a calm evening. Sanju was sitting on the living room sofa. Meetha was in the kitchen cleaning and washing the food equipment and organising things in a proper order. Lalit was at home, watching the news when suddenly the doorbell rang.

“I’ll get it,” Lalit said. He walked towards the door and opened it, surprised to see Mira Bhabhi standing with Nirmal by her side.

There was a sudden silence between the two brothers. Without a word, he let them in.

Mira came out from the kitchen wondering who it was. She was surprised to see the look on Lalit's face, one of confusion and silence.

They all sat on the sofa. Sanju greeted his uncle and aunty.

"I was wondering why Mira was mostly out of the house even after I could come home from work. Just two days ago, she told me everything. I didn't know all this was going on."

Lalit looked at Meetha, wondering what to say, "Meetha wanted to create another source of income. I supported her and Mira Bhabhi's idea."

"Hmm, I can see that all of this was going on behind my back but I understand why. Lalit, I have come to tell you," Nirmal, sitting across Lalit looking deep into his eyes, "that I am happy you were open to this idea."

Lalit was shocked at his brother's response, "You agree, bhaiya?"

"Why wouldn't I? When you turned down the idea of putting Ma and Baba's room on rent, I was worried about the way you thought. You no longer seemed like a person who was open to fresh ideas. I understand that it was our parent's room but we also needed the money. Just because I earn two times more than you do every month does not mean that we are better off. Earning and saving are two different things."

"I am sorry, bhaiya. Things really got out of hand between us. It is not what Ma and Baba would have wanted."

"It's okay. Mistakes were made on both sides. So, now that all this is out of the way, let's discuss how we want to do this. Let's work as a family. You, Meetha, and Sanju should come back because if we are going to do this together then it is better if we are living under one roof."

Meetha felt a wave of relief and a sudden bout of joy realising that they might be able to go back to things the way they were.

"Bhaiya, we would love that more than anything."

So, it was settled between the two brothers and both the families as a whole.

Nirmal contributed to creating separate savings for his wife and children, and for Lalit, Meetha, and Sanju through insurance plans. At the same time, Lalit and Meetha saved every penny they could to secure medical expenses for Sanju's treatment and education.

The seizures and its frequency reduced drastically as Sanju was back with his cousins.

Two years had passed. Meetha and Mira's business picked up gradually as they rented a small place to cook the food, homemade style and deliver dabbas through a delivery service.

They were able to raise funds after making a saving of at least three lakhs a year. They called their business '*Mira & Meetha's Homemade Kitchen*'. They allot close to Rs 200,000 per year on sales and marketing. It was not much but they decided to keep it at a bare minimum while their delivery man was paid an extra sum every month to distribute promotion pamphlets door-to-door.

Category	**Nirmal's contribution**	**Lalit & Meetha contribution**	**Total**
Savings for the family	Savings for wife and children	Savings for Sanju's medical expenses and education	Total family savings
Insurance plans	Insurance plans for Lalit, Meetha, and Sanju		Total insurance premium
Business expenses		Rental for kitchen, delivery service, sales and marketing, delivery man's salary	Total business expenses

- After deducting expenses, their business annual income: Rs 6,00,00 per year
- Their annual savings goal: Rs 3 lakhs per year
- Medical expenses for Sanju: Rs 1.5 lakhs per year (average, considering fluctuations)

So, the breakdown would be approximately:

Category	**Amount (INR)**
Annual income	6,00,000
Annual expenses	3,00,000 (including rent, utilities, food, etc.)
Annual savings	3,00,000
Annual medical expenses for Sanju	1,50,000
Savings for the future	1,50,000 (further divided into an education fund for Sanju, Emergency, and retirement fund)

"We're doing a good job with our savings." Lalit said at the family dinner table. "I'm just worried that we don't spread ourselves too thin on the cost of insurance premiums. It has reduced our disposable income."

A disposable income refers to the sum of money a person or a family can spend or save after taxes and other deductions.

"What if the income we get from the business fluctuates? We have to be ready for the unexpected like a year of losses, medical emergencies, house repairs, and so on." Lalit said as he chewed on his food.

"What if we put the second home on rent?" Meetha pointed out, "It would mean added work for us but it would also mean added income."

"It would be a steady flow of income." Nirmal agreed

"Yes, and seeing how none of us are living there, it would be a good source to depend on, especially in times of emergencies or when we don't make as much from the business in any particular year."

"What if we also steadily increase our menu price?"

So, Mira and Meetha increased their menu prices by 5% each year which cushioned their expenses for ingredients and the savings. They realised that every year, they must increase their menu prices as inflammation increases.

In addition, Lalit invested his savings into multiple fixed deposits, with each deposit accumulating over ₹50,000 in value. Among the fixed deposits he established, Lalit prematurely closed three at the end of three years, withdrawing ₹1.75 lakhs, which he then added to a mutual funds account.

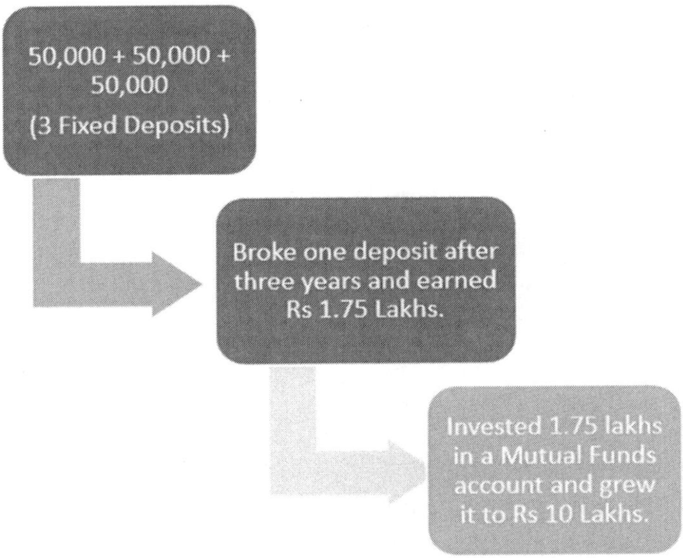

Use the table below to jot down:

- The **Types of Deposits/Accounts** you would want to create for the different goals of your life and/or your family's wellbeing.
- Feel free to **Add an Amount** you think you can put to each account on a per month or per year basis.
- Alternatively, you can put the **Figures You Want to Achieve** for each family member.

TYPES OF DEPOSITS / ACCOUNTS	**Family Member 1** (Name: - ________)	**Family Member 2** **(Name: -** ________)	**Family Member 3** (Name: - ________)
Deposit 1			
Deposit 2			
Deposit 3			
Recurring Deposit 1			
Recurring Deposit 2			
Mutual Funds Account			
Emergency Fund			

"Thanks for the suggestion bhaiya." Lalit and Meetha sat with Nirmal and Mira in the house. "It has been eight years now. If you had not suggested the mutual funds account idea, I would not be sitting here today with 10 lakhs worth of mutual fund assets alone apart from the other savings we have ."

"Keep saving as you go and see where we will reach as a family. Don't worry, we are all making adjustments. I am thinking now that Mira and Meetha have understood the ropes of how to manage their business, we should help them expand into another locality as well."

“Wow, I never thought we would reach this far already that now we are talking about expanding their business. It is a good idea. There will be a lot to do and we will need more people.” said Lalit

Meetha and Mira looked at each other, “Imagine, Mira Bhabhi. Both of us handle two branches.”

“You take one branch and I will take one.” Said Mira

“And I will cook in mummy’s kitchen.” Sanju said. Meetha looked at her son, admiring his bright smile, realising his future is more secure and free.

Five years flew by. Mira and Meetha worked hard to keep their business thriving. The expenses and savings were closely monitored by the four of them. Nirmal and Lalit made sure to support Mira and Meetha whenever they could. The mutual funds account that Lalit had invested in grew to 10 lakhs five years ago and went up to 20 lakhs.

Meetha was munching on two cheese spinach samosas that were left over from the day’s delivery. She had made a little extra, so she decided to have some with her evening cup of tea. Sanju was in his room, reading a book as he was trained in the support group. While he was about to turn a page, the corner of his eye caught a swift movement from the outside of his room. He rushed to check what had happened thinking someone or something fell to the floor.

Upon reaching his room door, he peeped out to see Mira bhabhi almost falling on his mother. Stepping out of his room, he saw his mother and aunt jumping in joy over a magazine. Meetha saw Sanju pop up between them to see what was happening. Meetha showed him a glossy page in the magazine that read - the top 10 Under 40s women business owners. Mira and Meetha’s Homemade Food made it to the 5th of the list.

Over the next few days, a wall in their living room saw a framed photo of an achievement they never believed to have achieved.

Sanju touched the framed magazine page, his fingers lingering over his mother's photo. "Mummy," he said softly, "you're a superhero."

Meetha laughed, but her tears fell anyway. For the boy who'd fought seizures. For the woman who'd once been too timid to speak. For the family that had fractured, then forged itself anew—not in gold, but in the humble steel of shared struggle.

Initial Financial Situation:

- **Financial Strain:** Significant financial strain due to Sanju's medical expenses and the family rift.
- **Limited Income:** Low income and potential job loss for Lalit.
- **Emergency Fund:** Lack of a substantial emergency fund.

Financial Strategies Implemented:

1. **Entrepreneurship:**
    - **Home-Based Business:** Meetha and Mira started a home-based food business, "Mira & Meetha's Homemade Kitchen."
    - **Initial Investment:** They used their savings and borrowed funds to start the business.
    - **Revenue Generation:** They generated revenue through sales to the support group and potential future customers.
2. **Financial Planning and Budgeting:**
    - **Budgeting:** They created a detailed budget to track income and expenses.
    - **Savings:** They allocated a portion of their income to savings and investments.
    - **Emergency Fund:** They started building an emergency fund to cover unexpected expenses.
3. **Investment Strategies:**
    - **Fixed Deposits:** Lalit invested in fixed deposits to earn interest.
    - **Mutual Funds:** He invested in mutual funds for long-term growth.
4. **Family Support and Collaboration:**
    - **Joint Venture:** Nirmal and Mira supported the business venture, potentially providing financial assistance and resources.
    - **Shared Expenses:** The families shared expenses and resources to reduce individual burdens.

5. **Business Expansion:**
   - **Scaling Up:** They planned to expand the business by renting a commercial kitchen and hiring more staff.
   - **Marketing and Sales:** They invested in marketing and sales strategies to attract more customers.

One-Minute Financial Hack!!!

Switch to a high-yield savings account - Research online banks offering 6-8% interest rates vs traditional 3-4%. Start the application today. Do your due diligence

Bonus: If you have a passion or skill that can be monetised . Start working on it now. Your retirement shall be more fulfilling than you thought .

Book club chat

- Do you think starting a business is a viable option to increase income and financial security?
- Were there other investment options that Lalit and Meetha along with Nirmal and Mira could opt for?
- What do you think about strong family bonds? Had Lalit not patched up with his brother Nimal, would they still be able to manage the family expenses individually?

Potential Financial Roadblocks and How to Handle Them

1. Business Fluctuations/Losses

- **Roadblock:** The income from "Mira & Meetha's Homemade Kitchen" could fluctuate or even face losses, as Lalit worried.
- **Resolution: Diversify income sources** (like renting out the second home), **maintain an emergency fund** to cover lean periods, and **adjust pricing regularly** to counter inflation and maintain profit margins.

2. Overspending on Insurance Premiums

- **Roadblock:** Lalit expressed concern that high insurance premiums could reduce their disposable income significantly.

- **Resolution: Regularly review insurance policies** to ensure they meet current needs without being excessive. Explore competitive family packages and term insurance options, balancing coverage with affordability.

3. Marketing & Expansion Costs

- **Roadblock:** Growing the business into new localities and effective marketing requires significant investment, which could deplete savings.
- **Resolution: Start small and scale gradually**, as they did with Avinash. Research cost-effective marketing strategies (like online content and local promotions), consider hiring freelancers for specific tasks, and continuously **reinvest a portion of profits** back into the business for sustainable growth.

Rathandeep's Kaleidoscope

Life throws curveballs, but your financial future doesn't have to crumble. As Meetha and Lalit discovered, **courage to act** on her talent , combined with **family support** and **disciplined planning**, can transform daunting challenges into remarkable achievements. Don't underestimate the power of **diverse income streams** and **smart savings**—they're your safety net and your launchpad to independence and shared prosperity.

Back in the garden

"You got featured in the business outlook magazine? Wow! That's amazing" said Damini "We're so proud of you Meetha. You and your bhabhi working together. It's hardly ever the case where two sister-in-laws get along so well."

"That was the happiest day of our lives since we started our business. It was a day to celebrate because after that day, we started to get more orders. In a year's time, we had opened our third branch."

"You are truly an inspiration, Meetha. I mean, to be featured in a magazine and then have your business pick up more after that is just like a dream come true."

"Well, that was my story and how we managed our money around it all." Getting a call on her mobile, Meetha saw Sanju calling her, "Well, ladies, next week then?"

"No, next week will feel like next year." said Bhavani, "I want to talk about my story and I can't wait. Let's meet tomorrow. All I will say for now is that my story began when I lost my grandmother over a silly family feud. That's where my ambition began."

"Oh, that's too bad, Bhavani." said Shivani, "Indeed, let's all try to meet tomorrow."

The ladies left for the night, and came back the next evening with a bunch of snacks and drinks. Our next story begins with Bhavani...

A SAFE HAVEN FOR THE ELDERLY AND A BABY ON THE WAY

PART 1

The blue glow of the phone illuminated Bhavani's face as she scrolled through Instagram in the silence of the night. Ravi, her husband, was out of town on an annual company trip. As she scrolled ahead from hilarious cat videos to zodiac memes, a sponsored ad popped up shattering the stillness.

> *In the guise of taking them on a pilgrimage to sacred places in India, many people drive and leave their parents in an unknown place in the middle of nowhere. The parents, the elderly, old mothers, and fathers, are left to fend for themselves with no place else to live or go back home. They are then left on the streets as homeless people, begging for food and shelter.*
>
> *It is a sorry state of the country where parents are given the position of Gods but are treated worse than enemies as they age.*
>
> *I have been working hard towards giving these helpless citizens a place to live in this old age home. As they are old, we often need medical assistance and an ambulance to transport them to a hospital. For this, I need...*

A stark plea for donations flashed below, urging viewers to support the organisation that cared for the elderly.

A lump formed in Bhavani's throat. Memories of her grandmother surfaced – the way her vibrant spirit dwindled as neglect chipped away at her, the helplessness Bhavani felt witnessing her grandmother's decline and ultimate demise. Back then, resources were scarce and so was awareness. The ad that broke into her night's sleep reignited a familiar ache, a yearning to do something, anything.

Another hour passed away as she dwelled deeper into the recesses of a known memory. Every unspoken word, every dilemma-filled approach, and every action not taken loomed before her eyes when tears started to well up. She remembers the first time she saw her grandmother dressed in skin and bones as opposed to the child-like love that adorned her smile.

"You can leave. We don't need you or your wife here. I am capable enough to take care of our mother." Said Bhavani's mother's elder brother

"We would like to meet Amma. What is wrong if we just come for a visit." Bhavani's father asked, struggling to understand the reason behind his brother-in-law's behaviour.

Bhavani held her mother's hand as she heard these vicious words come out of her uncle. Her cousin was in another room, not willing to come out and meet her. The memory was pure as daylight. She remembered how her uncle's wife remained indifferent to the state of affairs. She made sure that Nani (Bhavani's grandmother) didn't speak to them. Her form, frail and thin lay unmasked behind her smile.

Almost in tears, Bhavani, at the tender age of 13, was torn to pieces when she realised that her grandmother was neglected. She had grown old, giving her eldest son the worst of an excuse to not look after his own mother with dignity, love, and respect.

"I have come here to meet my mother. Why are you stopping us?" said Bhavani's mother

"I know why you all have come here. You can't take Amma from my house. She belongs here, so you have seen her now? She is fine, right? Now leave and don't come back again."

Puzzled at the way her brother spoke, Bhavani's mother sought to take her mother back to live with her in the coming weeks. Unfortunately, a few weeks later, news had arrived that her mother had passed away due to an underlying illness.

Even years later, Bhavani asks her mother why her uncle was so cruel.

"Why would they not give Nani three meals a day? Why just breakfast? Why would they not give her proper medications or pay for her medicines? This is not only neglect, this is murder, Ma."

"Bhavani, I don't want to talk about it. There is nothing I can do now. Just please, leave me in peace." Her mother would storm out of the room whenever Bhavani questioned her uncle's conduct. The guilt had driven her to the point of neglecting the topic altogether.

Her Nani's photo on the wall was a stark reminder of the woman who was loved by her granddaughter and will always be cherished. As the long-held memory wore her down, sleep started to set in, and she drifted until the early morning hours.

Six hours later, morning rays crept into her room. Bhavani awoke on the weekend. Ravi was going to be home around noon returning from a company trip. She knew he would have to shake off the sleepiness to attend a relative's wedding reception.

While the thoughts of last night still haunted her, the day had just begun with a new chapter about to unfold.

"I can't stop yawning." Said Ravi still sleepy from the company trip

"It's okay" Bhavani looks for a parking space as they approach the wedding reception venue, "I am sure it will all be over soon."

"Don't fall asleep Ravi. These company trips… Why do you go every year?" Ravi's father asked with an almost irritated tone.

"Papa, you know how it is; you have to go on these trips. It's a great way for…"

"You don't have to tell me. I know, I worked in a company for 45 years. They never did all this drama. Take trips and waste money. Why not just give that money to you and the other employees?"

"Yes, papa, you are right but times have changed." a splash of regret hits Ravi's face wondering why he agreed to attend the wedding reception in the first place.

Bhavani finds a good parking space, "Okay, let's not forget anything." They all get out of the car. Bhavani helps her mother-in-law step out of the car while she helps her carry her purse.

"Bhavani, you didn't forget the house keys, no?"

"No, amma, I did not forget. They are the first thing I put in my purse."

"Okay, good. You remember I told you about your father-in-law when he was in a hurry to go to his nephew's wedding?"

"Yes, amma."

They walked towards the entrance, a far walk from the car parked in a shaded place.

"Yes, yes. I forgot the house keys. Six years, and she never fails to remind me." Says Bhavani's father-in-law.

"Did you bring the house keys today?" asks the Bhavani's mother-in-law even though she knew the answer.

"Bhavani has carried the house keys. Why should I carry a spare?"

"Can't expect anything from you. At least my daughter-in-law remembered. By the way, I carried a spare set of keys."

They entered the venue after finding a parking space amid the rows of cars lined up like a car sale. A large reception with people standing at the entrance greeting the guests. Bhavani and Ravi look for a table. Realising they should have reached an hour earlier; their eyes desperately search for a vacant table. Finally, they find one in the corner with an old couple sitting and eating the appetisers. Six chairs surrounded the table, generously spaced apart from each other. The old couple occupied two chairs, leaving four for Bhavani, Ravi, and his parents.

Giving each other a soft glance and a smile, Bhavani, Ravi and his parents sit next to the old couple. Waiters walk around offering snacks and drinks to every guest. Bhavani looks for the newlyweds and finds them standing on the stage receiving gifts, envelopes, awkward jokes, and endless jaw-aching smiles. Soon Bhavani, Ravi, and his parents had to partake in the same façade.

After their lineup at the buffet section, they sat at the table with their plates. The old couple who was sitting had already brought their food. They smiled at Bhavani and Ravi while their glances fell on the perceived void between them, or so they imagined. Bhavani was able to guess what they were thinking and knew the words ahead of their silence were about to turn into an awkward conversation.

"How long have you both been married?" Asked the old man

Ravi looked up from his plate. "5 years" stuffing food into his mouth, ready to eat, finish, and leave.

"No children?"

PART 2

The next morning was a peaceful break from the wedding reception.

"You saw the way Papa defended their question? As though we don't care at all about anything. Why did he have to say it like that – *'Oh, children? Tough chance with these two!'* I mean, why?" Ravi imitates his father while folding the sheets on the bed.

"We could probably plan for a baby in the coming year," Bhavani said while getting ready for work.

"I don't know. Yes, maybe. Why not? I believe it will be easier after my boss agrees on an increment. Frankly speaking, bringing up the topic with him is getting harder and harder. It feels like I am talking to my father where the answer to every question is *NO*."

"Whatever it is, we will deal with it together." Bhavani smiles at Ravi hoping to give him some respite from the pressure they both felt.

"Yes… we will." Ravi smiles back, "You know, if Amma and Papa just realised how times have changed. Expenses have increased so much that even having one baby turns into a big decision. These days when I come across schools that charge lakhs per year for a school fee, I wonder whether we will be able to sustain even one child's education."

Ravi's fear was valid. Bhavani too felt helpless, swimming between two shores of an unspoken ambition and the need to plan a family.

"I will go for a shower now and get ready for work. Should I drop you today?" Ravi asks

"Yes, I would like that…"

"How is your work these days?" Ravi asks Bhavani while driving her to work.

"It's good. There's never a dull moment in HR! We had a few interview schedules clashing last week but we sorted it out."

Bhavani's phone rings, "Smita?"

Ravi looks at Bhavani while at the wheel. She answers the call.

"Hello?... Hi… Yes, hi Smita. How are you? Arrey, no way… how could I forget? But yes, it's been so many years."

Ravi listened on as Bhavani spoke to her friend. After a few minutes, she hangs up the call.

"Old friend?"

"We interned together at the same institute. This was at least seven to eight years ago. Surprised that she would invite me."

"Invite you?"

"She is hosting a charity event for blind children and she has invited me to attend. Do you think I should go? I told her I would let her know."

"When is it?"

"It's two weeks from now. Saturday. The event starts at 6.00 pm."

"Is it far?"

"I don't know. She said she would send the details."

"Well, if you want you could go. I mean, why not? I always have late afternoon shifts on Saturdays, so I won't be able to join you but you could go and see what it is all about."

***

Two weeks fly by and Bhavani finds herself standing outside a bustling community centre, the venue for Smita's charity event. The late afternoon sun casts long shadows, painting the building in a warm glow. Upbeat music spills out through the open doors, a mix of traditional and contemporary tunes. A colourful banner hangs above the entrance, proclaiming *"Light up Their World: A Charity Event for Blind Children."*

As Bhavani approaches, she sees a flurry of activity. Volunteers in bright t-shirts with the event logo scurry around, carrying boxes and setting up tables. Parents arrive with their children, some holding onto colourful balloons or small stuffed animals. The air buzzes with a mix of excitement and anticipation.

Taking a deep breath, Bhavani steps through the doorway. The interior is a kaleidoscope of sights and sounds. Tables are laden with brightly coloured cupcakes, cookies, and other treats. A makeshift stage sits at the far end, decorated with balloons and streamers.

Children, some with white canes or guide dogs, explore the space, their laughter echoing the walls.

She spots Smita near the entrance, registering attendees. Still as energetic and friendly as she was seven to eight years ago. Welcoming her with a warm hug, "Bhavs, so glad you could make it! Let me get you registered."

"Glad to be here, Smita." Bhavani signs the register of attendees, "So great to see you after such a long time. You've outdone yourself here."

"Thank you so much, Bhavs. Come, let me help you get seated."

Bhavani follows Smita, taking her to sit comfortably at a place where every part of the event would be visible. Volunteers are assisting children with painting and craft activities. Everywhere she looks, she sees smiles and a sense of community. The joy on the children's faces is infectious, and a heartwarming feeling washes over her. "This is clearly more than just a fundraiser, it's like the coming together of a community." Bhavani points out to Smita.

"I can't agree more. I worked very hard for this despite my job. I just hope today becomes a success. Society needs to come together for these children. They have been long neglected, especially those from the lower sections of society."

Finally bringing Bhavani to her designated seat, Smita promises to meet her after the event has ended.

As the evening unfolds, she is struck by a calling that goes beyond her. A higher ambition that she has been contemplating for a long time, and she wonders to herself whether this charity event was just the nudge she needed:

She watched the final act on stage, a group of blind children performing a heart-tugging skit on friendship and acceptance. The audience erupted in applause, tears glistening in some eyes. As the crowd began to disperse, Bhavani found Smita by a table stacked with leftover treats.

"Smita," Bhavani began, her voice hesitant, "this event was incredible. The way you brought everyone together... It was truly inspiring."

Smita beamed, "Thanks, Bhavs. It means a lot coming from you. But you know, it wasn't easy. If I wasn't still working in HR and doing this on the side, it would still take up a lot of my time. Finding sponsors, and coordinating with volunteers, takes up a significant amount of my time. But I am passionate about it."

"I bet it does. It makes me wonder... if you could pull this off, of course through immense hard work, which is quite evident here... what if I too could do something I've been wanting to do for a long time?"

Smita raised an eyebrow, intrigued, "What do you mean?"

"Remember how I told you about my grandmother and how she passed away?"

Smita's smile softened, "Yes, I remember. It was just heartbreaking, Bhavs."

"Well, today's event sparked something in me. I want to help the elderly who have been abandoned by their children, forgotten, and just left to fend for themselves. I was thinking maybe I could open a home. A place they would be cared for, and not just a home, but to also spread awareness for those who can identify whether or not their children are treating them well."

"That's a great idea, Bhavs. But it's a huge undertaking, you will need funding, a facility, staff…"

"I know, I know. It's a lot. But seeing the impact of your event today just reinforces my belief that I can do something too. But I need your guidance. What do you say?"

"Hmm…" Smita thinks for a while and then smiles at Bhavani, "Okay, let's take this one step at a time. How about we meet next week, brainstorm some ideas, and see where it goes?"

"Absolutely!" Bhavani was filled with excitement, "I can't wait to talk about it with you."

They clasped hands, and a silent pact formed between two friends. Bhavani couldn't wait to tell Ravi about her long and awaited ambition.

PART 3

Bhavani hummed along the radio as she drove home, a lightness dancing in her chest. The conversation with Smita had ignited a fire within her, a sense of purpose she hadn't felt in a long time. Pulling into the driveway, she noticed the familiar blue sedan in the parking lot. Ravi had reached home.

Stepping inside, she found Ravi sprawled on the couch, the TV flickering silently in the background. He looked exhausted, dark circles smudging his usually bright eyes.

"Hey," Bhavani greeted softly, setting her bag down, "how was work today?"

“Ravi shifted, a groan escaping his lips, “It was okay. There were a lot of orders to process and document. They want me to complete everything, so I have to put in a 14-hour shift tomorrow… on a Sunday. Can you believe this?”

Bhavani winced, “Oh, that sounds awful. Here, let me get you some water.”

“It’s okay, I already had some.”

“Have some more.” She returned with a glass, watching Ravi as he took a long swig. The exhaustion seemed to weigh him down, pulling energy out of the room.

“Actually,” Bhavani started hesitatingly, “there is something I wanted to talk to you about.”

His eyes glued to the television screen. Another groan slips from his lips, “Sure, what is it?”

Taking a deep breath, Bhavani recounted the events of the evening, starting with Smita’s charity event and ending their discussion about opening a home for the elderly. As she spoke, Ravi slowly started to sit up, curiosity flickering in his eyes. Suddenly, the TV screen seemed less distracting. His expression shifted from mild interest to surprise and then a touch of concern.

“A home for the elderly? Bhavani?” a worried tone in his voice. “That’s a big… big idea.”

“I know,” she admitted, “but seeing those kids today, the way Smita brought everyone together… it just made me realise I want to do something similar, something bigger, more permanent.”

Ravi tapped his fingers against the armrest. “It’s noble, sweetheart, truly. But it’s also a huge commitment. A lot of work, a lot of responsibility.”

Bhavani nodded, her smile unwavering, “I know, and I wouldn’t take it lightly. But wouldn’t it be amazing, Ravi? To create a place for those who have been forgotten, to give them a home of dignity and respect in their golden years? For so long, I have regretted the passing of my grandmother. I cannot carry that regret with me for the rest of my life without doing anything about it. Believe me, I have been feeling very strongly about this, more than I have ever shared with you."

A flicker of doubt crossed Ravi's face. "I understand, Bhavani. Many times, you discussed your grandmother with me, and I know what you have been feeling about it for a long time. But doing this sounds like a lot to handle. We have been talking about starting a family ourselves and with your job, and this project…"

Bhavani reached out, placing her hand on his arm, "I know what we've been talking about Ravi. But this doesn't have to replace it. Maybe… maybe we can do both. Maybe this could even be a part of our future family, a way to share our lives with those who need it the most."

Ravi studied his wife's words and expressions for a moment, doubt battled with a spark of admiration in his eyes. "We'd need a solid plan, Bhavani. We would need to figure out finances, logistics, everything. And it wouldn't be easy."

"I know it wouldn't." She readily agreed, "But wouldn't it be worth it, Ravi? To leave a mark, to make a difference in the lives of others?"

Ravi fell silent, lost in thought. He realised how strongly she felt about this matter. The weight of her words hung in the air with heavy potential and challenge. He noticed a profound determination shining in her eyes. In that moment, he saw not just his wife, but a woman ignited by a cause.

"Okay," he finally said, a slow smile spreading across his face. *"Maybe this is how we parent before we're parents—by learning to care for those no one else will."*"Let's talk about a plan. We can figure this out together. Maybe this crazy idea of yours isn't so crazy after all."

Bhavani's heart soared. This wasn't just her dream anymore, it was theirs. She clapped her hands in excitement.

"First! We will discuss it and see whether it is feasible. I am not promising anything." Ravi held her hands so that she understood that this kind of family project must be taken one step at a time. "If we don't see things going in the right direction and it is too much for us to handle, we will have to make another serious decision as to whether it is right to continue this work or not. Understood?"

"Yes, understood." Silently, she hoped that it would never come to that!

Did you have dreams to better this world and do you think those dreams were too big to dream? Would they need a lot of from your to do it
Send us your thoughts by scanning this QR Code.Lets see where the strength of collective vibration leads us to?

PART 4

The weight of the decision settled on Bhavani and Ravi's shoulders comfortably, a shared burden that felt lighter than the weight of their unspoken dreams. The weekend stretched before them, a canvas for planning and strategising.

The following weekend when Ravi had an additional day off due to last week's double shift, they had the time to think together. Bhavani met Smita in the past week to get all the insights and guidance she could. The time for planning, putting pen to paper, and critical evaluations had arrived.

So, Bhavani and Ravi began pulling out their laptops and opening spreadsheets across the dining table. A shared document titled "Project Golden Years Haven" became their battleground. Bhavani listed down the initial costs, renting or purchasing a facility, basic amenities, medical supplies, staff salaries, and utilities. Ravi meticulously analysed their current income and expenses, factoring in potential loan options and long-term sustainability.

"We can definitely manage a decent initial investment," Ravi declared, tapping away at the keyboard. "But for ongoing expenses, especially staffing, we might need to find alternative income streams."

Bhavani mulled it over. Fundraising? Grants? Maybe even approaching NGOs for collaboration?

Listing down the initial costs for Golden Years Haven, a familiar pang shot through her. Nestled between "medical supplies" and "staff salaries," she wrote down "child education fund", and "Child's overall expenses."

Ravi, catching her thoughtful expression, gently touched her hand. "We can factor in future expenses for a little one too," he said reassuringly.

They both knew that raising a child would be a significant financial commitment. Balancing the project's needs with their own growing family would require careful planning and adjustments.

Later that evening, after a productive brainstorming session for fundraising ideas for the project, they revisited the personal side of their family plan.

"Maybe we can set up a separate savings account for the baby's education." Bhavani suggested, "Even a small amount each month will add up over time. Let us add Rs 30,000 every month. So, you add fifteen thousand and I will add fifteen thousand."

Ravi nodded, "Yes, so that would be regarding the savings for our child's education. Apart from that, we could also start sifting through some good health insurance covers. I will also research childcare options. Depending on our work schedules and the project's needs, we might need to factor in daycare or nanny costs."

Bhavani thought for a while and then remembered Smita's approach, "Smita didn't start immediately. She created a separate account saving money every year. Finally, when she gathered the funds she required, she launched her project."

"So, when did she really start?"

"She started after four years."

"Okay, fair enough." Ravi said, "Our project is also a huge undertaking but if we have enough funds, we can also approach investors and banks. We have to compute how much we would need for this project."

"Smita gave me the number of a social entrepreneur who helped her decide the capital she required. Let's talk to him."

They could envision the temporary adjustments they would have to make but felt confident to navigate them together.

Ravi and Bhavani sat across a table in a compact office with a man named Gopal Bakshi, the social entrepreneur recommended by Smita.

"What is your experience in elder care?" Gopal asked

"Well," Bhavani said, "We never really had any experience before of taking care of the elderly in a home. We are not sure how to go about this but I have a fair idea from Smita."

"Yes, Smita indeed has experience but her area is different. She is looking after the welfare, wellbeing, and future of blind children who are abandoned by society. In your case, you wish to take care of the elderly. Now, remember that if things don't work out or seem too overwhelming, you cannot give up. This is a social cause, you will be causing further abandonment of these poor souls if you give up in the middle. Is that understood?"

Bhavani and Ravi looked at each other, and then at Gopal, "We understand. Why would we give up?" Ravi asked

"People in our level of society are used to working hard for ourselves and our own. With the daily struggles, we barely have time to look out for other people. Tell me, on your way here, how many homeless people did you notice on the streets?"

Bhavani and Ravi were unable to answer.

"Okay, let's see you'll notice 50 homeless people on the sidewalks. How many of them were among the elderly?"

There was an awkward silence between them.

"Don't worry about my questions. I ask them so that you know where you stand. Before you can begin this project, understand that you are the parents of the elderly. When you have a child, if they do something wrong, or they are being stubborn, or you can't make their lives easier, will you leave them on the streets? Similarly, when it comes to the elderly, they will need expensive medical care that many times, you both will not be able to provide. That is the time, you will require funds because for the elderly, time is of the essence."

Bhavani remembered the video she watched on Instagram. The plea back then too seemed desperate. For a moment, she started to wonder, would she and Ravi be able to pull it off? Was she jumping into this project too soon?

"You will always have doubts, and every night will be either something you are looking forward to or are worried will happen.

But I am here to tell you all of that which you too will experience will be normal. All I am asking is that first the two of you need to work on your mindset. This undertaking is a huge responsibility which I will help you with, so you don't have to feel like you are alone or need to give up."

A wave of relief passed over Bhavani and Ravi. Knowing they were not alone was something they wanted to hear during this meeting.

"When it comes to a large-scale nursing home, the investment can be in tens of crores. So, in your case since you both are also planning a family at the same time, let us start with a few lakhs to start building up for a small-scale home-based care. So, for the next three to four years, just keep building up your savings for this project."

"What should be our goal for how much we need to save each year?"

"For each year alone, aim for 15 lakh rupees. By the end two years, you will have saved thirty lakhs. With thirty lakhs as your savings, apply for a bank loan to rent a place where you can bring elderly people. Start with one elderly person after two years, see how you are able to manage with one elderly person. Six months later, add another, and then another. Keep only three elderly people and one caretaker."

"Ravi earns Rs 1,75,000 and I earn Rs 50,000 every month. From our earnings, we will be able to save Rs 100,000 every month."

"Make some efforts to allocate Rs 75,000 every month into a mutual funds account. Grow it for a specific number of years. This will help grow your savings exponentially. Don't just depend on mutual funds, try renting out a place if possible so you can get some additional income from somewhere. If that is not possible then based on your career expertise, open a small consulting business and earn a side income from the same."

One evening, while at the dinner table, Bhavani and Ravi invited their parents and Bhavani's parents to discuss their dream. They anticipated scepticism, perhaps even disapproval, given the scale of the project.

"Look, it's a good thought and I understand your intentions, but I think you both are biting off more than you can chew." Said Ravi's father

"Ravi, your father is right," Bhavani's father agreed, "Have you considered how this can affect your chances of raising a child and doing this project simultaneously? The world is a cruel place and people get abandoned, be it a child or an old man or woman. Does that mean you have to solve all the world's problems?"

The words that Bhavani and Ravi had to hear were something they anticipated but were still difficult to tackle. They realised it would have been better to complete their dinner and then start the discussion. Alas, the cat was already out of the bag.

"Bhavani, you need to stop all of this madness and focus on your plan to become a mother. This is not the right time to think about all of this." Bhavani's mother said with a concerned tone

An overwhelming wave of emotion took hold of Bhavani as she recalled how her mother always shut her out whenever she tried to talk about her grandmother.

"Then when Ma? When would be a good time? Can you please tell me or should I keep quiet about this too?"

"Don't you understand? It is like what your father said, you can't help everyone."

"No, Ma. I could not help my grandmother." Bhavani's words resounded across the table, "But I can help people who are in a similar condition like her or worse."

"Please! Don't make this about your grandmother?" Bhavani's mother raised her voice by a decibel

"Okay, then… let me make it about your mother. She was your mother. Could you have not done something? Does it never occur to you that Nani may have needed help but your brother just neglected her, and why? Why was she living there like a hostage?"

"I don't have to listen to this… We did all we could to bring her back but it was complicated. You were too young to understand all of this!"

"You never want to talk about Nani who was so important to me. And now, even today, you can't support a decision Ravi and I made together."

"Let someone who has the finances do this… someone who does not have a family. They have fewer responsibilities. Why do you both have to take this load upon yourselves? Is this all really necessary?" Ravi's father intervened only to add fuel to Bhavani's fiery eyes which were already tearing up.

Ravi gently squeezed Bhavani's hand at the table before she could say anything else. "Look, we called you all here tonight to have a peaceful discussion but I guess it is only fair that you'll have your doubts and apprehensions about our decision." Ravi looked around the table and his parents and then at Bhavani's, "It is not going to be easy but we have been planning our way ahead. All we ask is that you trust us."

The air at the table turned silent. Bhavani's mother nodded her head in disapproval. The fathers kept munching on their food. The only parent who had not yet spoken sat with her hands clasped under her chin. She looked around, first at all the parents, at Ravi, and then at Bhavani.

Feeling the tears flow from her daughter-in-law's eyes, she said, "I think you all should be proud of what a noble thing our children are planning to do."

Everyone looked up from their plates. "Kishore," turning to her husband sitting next to her, "You say that they are biting off more than they can chew but if it is something they firmly believe in then let them go ahead and see how it works."

"But life is not that simple. There are charitable organisations to do this. Ravi and Bhavani don't need to make life difficult, more than it already is."

"I think we should be more accepting of what they are trying to do, and it's for a good cause that very few people think of doing."

"Well, I am not going to encourage them to do this. I am going to forget this discussion ever happened." Said Ravi's father

"I am not surprised. Of course, it would be easy for you to forget things. This would be just another forgetful event on your list." Bhavani's mother-in-law winks at her, trying to lighten the mood at the table.

"Again with the house keys! Let it go already."

Bhavani's mother gets up from the table and walks away.

The night ended on an unresolved note.

Two and half years had passed by under the massive undertaking of endless paperwork and planning.

Bhavani and Ravi have accumulated and continued to save a defined percentage of money from their collective income. With thirty lakhs saved, they applied for a bank loan to operate a place to accommodate at least ten elderly people. As the social entrepreneur advised them to only bring in one elderly, they started with just one.

A **bank loan** is a financial product offered by banks that allows individuals or businesses to borrow a specific amount of money for a defined period. In return, the borrower agrees to pay back the principal amount, along with interest, in instalments or a lump sum.

In the context of their charitable venture, Bhavani and Ravi used a bank loan to acquire a suitable property to house the elderly individuals they planned to care for. Furthermore, they used the loan to renovate the property, making it suitable for elderly care, including necessary amenities and safety features.

The loan helped cover initial expenses like hiring staff, purchasing supplies, and paying utilities.

Other Uses of Bank Loans for Charitable ventures:

Bank loans can be a valuable tool for charitable organisations and social enterprises to achieve their goals. Here are some other potential uses:

1. **For Building and Infrastructure:**
2. **Purchasing Equipment and Technology:**
3. **Working capital Requirements**
4. **Operational Costs:**

It's important to note that when applying for a bank loan for a charitable organisation, it's crucial to have a solid business plan, demonstrating financial viability and social impact. Additionally, many banks offer special loan programs and interest rates for non-profit organisations and social enterprises. Or else, you may have to consider taking loan in personal name and repay through your earnings

What goals in your life do you think a bank loan can help you achieve?

Life Goal 1 (Ex:- Dream Car)	**Life Goal 2**	**Life Goal 3**

Need help understanding the necessary requirements for a bank loan and how to get it approved for you based on your life goals?

Scan this code to join my community.

At the same time, they reached Rs 3,60,000 by the end of two years for their 10-month-old daughter. "Let's continue to save our money for her," said Bhavani, "It has not been easy, Ravi. Without you, I don't know whether I could get this far." Baby Shreya had become a true source of happiness at home.

Ravi smiled at Bhavani. They sat at the bank waiting for the loan officer to bring the papers to sign some documents. "We are lucky to have parents who are supporting us despite their initial apprehensions. We have a lot of people with us; Smita, Mr Gopal, and yes, you too have worked very hard. You work during the day and also practise consultation in the evenings. Then we both take turns at night to take care of Shreya when she cries at night. It's been tiring. I could fall asleep right now if the loan officer does not come back immediately."

Bhavani laughs with Ravi, "Before going back home, let's go and take a quick nap in the car."

"Here are your papers, let me arrange them before signing." The loan officer came just in time.

The couple had already started with a life insurance plan, a health insurance cover, and other accounts opened for emergency funds to nest eggs were planned and adopted. Apart from this, Smita helped Bhavani and Ravi with various ways and ideas to continue building their project on Golden Years Haven. They met with Mr Gopal frequently to further plan and organise other ways to expand their project.

Bhavani would hold workshops to spread awareness of the importance of communication and nurturing between a person and their parents. One afternoon, Bhavani received a call from Smita. Ravi saw Bhavani rushing to him after the call. Her voice tinged with excitement. "There's been a development," she announced. "The local government is looking to partner with NGOs for a project related to senior care facilities. As founders of the Golden Years Haven Project, Smita thinks we could be the perfect fit."

Ravi's heart leaped. Six years had passed and project Haven was already housing fifteen elderly people. This was a game-changer, a potential solution to their funding woes and a chance to collaborate with other organisations with similar goals.

Bhavani's desire to fulfil her ambition for the elderly was finally taking its course. She would look at her grandmother's photo on the wall, hoping that she made her proud. With every penny saved and every calculated expense made, her project was coming through.

Amid all the adjustments, sticking to the plans of budgeting and raising a child, Bhavani and Ravi had grown to understand the significance of managing their money. They sensed a true calling towards making a difference in society while also experiencing a fulfilling family life with their daughter.

Together, Ravi and Bhavani converted their initial savings into long-term over the years:

Short-Term Savings:

- **Emergency Fund:** This fund is crucial for unexpected expenses like medical emergencies or job losses.
- **Child's Education Fund:** A dedicated fund for their child's future education, including tuition fees and other expenses.
- **Home Improvement Fund:** A fund to cover potential home renovations or repairs.

Long-Term Investments:

- **Fixed Deposits:** A reliable investment option with fixed interest rates.
- **Mutual Funds:** A diversified investment option with potential for higher returns.
- **Real Estate:** Investing in real estate can provide rental income and long-term appreciation.

Specific Savings Goals:

- **Golden Years Haven Project:** Initially, they saved Rs. 30 lakhs for the project's initial setup.
- **Child's Education:** They allocated Rs. 15,000 per month for their child's education fund.
- **Retirement:** They likely started saving for their retirement

- **Insurance:** They had life insurance, health insurance, and potentially other insurance policies to protect their family's financial security.
- **Tax Planning:** They may have consulted with a tax advisor to optimise their tax liabilities and maximise savings.
- **Debt Management:** They ensured they managed their debts responsibly, avoiding excessive borrowing.

Five years later, Bhavani completes a two-day workshop to a large group of younger people, both singles and families, about the relevance of caring for the elderly, "*It's not just us who matter but those who came before us as well. If they are ignored, what have we truly achieved and what does it say about us? Giving them a good life after their prime and making sure they can confidently look forward to a promising age in their golden years is what will eliminate so many of the troubles and challenges they go through silently...*"

The auditorium buzzed as Bhavani finished her elder care workshop. Spotting an elderly woman in the front row—her grandmother's mirror image—she stepped down, heart pounding.

"Your family?" Bhavani asked softly, nodding at the woman's faded face..

"They are abroad," the woman whispered. "Just money left."

Behind them, Shreya sprinted over, thrusting her strawberry ice cream at the stranger. "For you, Dadi-ma! Like Mummy's grandma loved it!"

Bhavani froze. She'd never told Shreya that detail.

The woman's eyes welled as she hugged Shreya. "She'd be proud," she murmured to Bhavani.

Outside, rain began to fall—washing the streets clean as Shreya skipped ahead, humming

- **Project Budget:** Created a detailed budget for the Golden Years Haven project, including initial investment, recurring expenses, and potential future costs.

- **Personal Finance:** Developed a personal budget to track income, expenses, and savings.
- **Emergency Fund:** Established an emergency fund to cover unexpected expenses.
- **Savings:** Consistently saved a portion of their income for the project and personal goals.
- **Investment:** Invested in mutual funds and other instruments for long-term growth.
- **Loan :** Secured a bank loan to finance the initial investment for the project.
- **Fundraising:** Explored fundraising opportunities, such as grants and donations.
- **Part-Time Income:** Considered part-time consulting work to supplement their income.
- **Financial Planning:** Consulted with a financial advisor to create a comprehensive financial plan.
- **Family Planning:** Planned for a child while balancing the demands of the project.
- **Childcare:** Considered childcare options and budgeted for related expenses.
- **Work-Life Balance:** Struggled to balance work and family commitments, especially during the initial stages of the project.
- **Retirement:** Planned for their own retirement, ensuring financial security for themselves and their family.
- **Business Expansion:** Considered future expansion of the Golden Years Haven project, including additional facilities and services.
- **Succession Planning:** Discussed potential succession plans for the business, especially in case of unforeseen circumstances.

One-Minute Financial Hack!!!

"The Ripple Round-Up"

- Activate round-up on payments apps
- Auto-invest the difference in: 70% index funds (your growth) 30% impact bonds (community growth)

Book Club Chats

- Do you think their decision to balance family life and social impact is realistic?
- What challenges do you think they might face in the future?
- If you were in their position, what would you do differently?

Potential Financial Roadblocks - How to Handle

1. High Initial Capital for Social Ventures

- **Roadblock:** Starting a large-scale project like "Golden Years Haven" requires significant initial capital (tens of crores for a large nursing home).
- **Resolution: Start small and scale gradually.** Bhavani and Ravi were advised to save for 3-4 years to accumulate an initial **₹30 lakhs** for a small-scale home, then expand incrementally, learning to manage with one elderly person before adding more. This de-risks the venture.

2. Balancing Personal Financial Goals with a Charitable Project

- **Roadblock:** The challenge of funding a large social project while simultaneously saving for personal milestones like a child's education and retirement.
- **Resolution: Integrate and prioritize goals with clear allocations.** Bhavani and Ravi set aside a dedicated amount for their child's education monthly (₹30,000) alongside their project savings. They also prioritized insurance and emergency funds, ensuring personal security wasn't compromised.

3. Securing Long-Term Funding and Sustainability for a Social Enterprise

- **Roadblock:** The ongoing operational costs, medical expenses for the elderly, and potential fluctuations in income for a charitable venture.
- **Resolution: Diversify funding sources.** They explored bank loans for property, and later sought **government partnerships** and **NGO collaborations**. Additionally, they considered side incomes like **consulting businesses** and possibly **renting out properties** to create steady alternative revenue streams.

Rathandeep's Kaleidoscope

Building a meaningful life, whether through personal aspirations or social impact, demands **audacious dreams paired with meticulous financial planning.** Bhavani and Ravi's journey shows that even the ambitious goals, like creating a haven for the elderly, are achievable through **disciplined savings, strategic investments (like mutual funds), and the courage to adapt and seek expert guidance.** Embrace challenges as opportunities for growth, because true wealth lies not just in accumulation, but in the purposeful pursuit of a fulfilling future aligned to your version of good life

Back in the garden

"Wow, you really made an impact, Bhavani. That's incredible." Sita said

"Yes, there's no doubt that your grandmother would be so proud of you. I am sure she blessed you even more." Shivani said

"Thank you so much, it means so much to me. Ravi and I worked very hard and seeing it come alive brought tears to our eyes that day."

"We have a lot to learn from you. I mean," Geetha continued, "For me, just planning and managing money for my family was exhausting enough. You raised a family and also did something so meaningful for the elderly. You are our inspiration for the day, Bhavani."

"Oh, wow. That means a lot but don't crown me just yet. We have our other two ladies who have yet to tell their stories to us. So who should we start with next?" asked Bhavani

They all coincidentally looked at Shivani, "Oh, me? Yes, sure... my story... well." Shivani thought for a while, "For me, everything started after everything ended..."

FROM DEPENDENCE TO INDEPENDENCE ON A JOURNEY TO SELF-BELIEF

PART 1

"Your life will be empty. And at 36? Have you thought about what will happen when you grow old?" Shivani patiently listened to a relative over the phone.

The phrase 'empty' echoed in her head.

"Someone's at the door, uncle. I will have to call you back." Shivani hung up before any other word or silence was exchanged. Sitting on the sofa in her parent's house, she looked blankly at the wall, almost zoning out from the noises in her head.

"Who was it today?" her mother asked, bringing a tray with two cups of warm milk. The aroma of jaggery and malai filled their living room. “This week, you have used the doorbell excuse at least a dozen times.”

“Ma, everyone talks to me like I have not thought this through? It’s like no one can see me for me but just the ‘divorce’ label on my forehead.”

Her mother placed the tray on the table before them and sat beside her.

“I got married without hesitation. Whatever dad said, who he chose. I didn’t ask too many questions. I really thought Gaurav was a good guy. Is this all my fault? I understand that ending a marriage is not a joke. But… does everyone think I am enjoying this? Where were they when Gaurav was misbehaving with me? Where were they on those nights when I would call you, crying over the telephone because of the huge fight he and his parents would have with me? Now suddenly, they all appear one after the other to talk me out of a divorce.”

Placing her hand on Shivani’s palm, her mother said, “If you keep thinking about what other people are saying then you will ruin your peace of mind. You have to be strong now and think about your future and the future of your children.” Her mother offers her the cup of milk, “Now have some warm milk and relax.”

Just then, Shivani’s 10-year-old daughter, Ankita, came into the living room, “Mumma, is Papa going to have dinner with us today?

Choking back her tears and forcing a smile, Shivani says, “Papa is at the office, Akku. He will be working late today.”

“Why does Papa work late every day?”

“Go, play in your room. Mumma will come and play with you.”

Ankita goes into her room, leaving Shivani and her mother back to their conversation.

Earlier that morning, the lawyer’s words echoed in Shivani’s head, a dull ache settling in her chest. “Divorce can be filed next week,

Shivani. We'll ensure a fair settlement..." But fair for whom? Gaurav, with his booming business and a knack for turning every deal into gold? Shivani, a school counsellor with a salary that barely covered groceries and the occasional movie ticket for Sayali and Ankita?

The past year had been a blur of arguments turning into fights, Gaurav's silences growing longer, and his presence a constant weight in their once vibrant home. The decision to divorce was fueled by a yearning for respect and a life where she wasn't constantly walking on eggshells. But now, a new fear gnawed at her – the fear of uncertainty.

"You think you can live without me? Who will provide for you? You can't rely on your parents forever. You're just a counsellor. If you're so smart, why don't you leave us? Let me see how long you'll last."

Words that cut like sharp razors kept Shivani awake at night. Gaurav's tone felt so different from when they had married 18 years ago. How could a person change so much and become so hateful? Or did Shivani fail to recognise him all these years? Her eyes met the dark ceiling in the room, staring at the fan's blades slicing through the air and her dreams of growing old with a trusted and loving life partner.

A gentle nudge against her stomach. Ankita clung to her mother. Shivani knew that the children had sensed something was amiss.

Her gaze fell upon Sayali, her elder daughter, fast asleep on the other side of the bed. From the age of 9 when all the chaos began. Now, at the delicate age of 14, she has grown beyond her years. Knowing too much, more than any fights between parents that a child should have to see. Sayali always protected Ankita from what she witnessed happening against me, and yet had to see it herself. Those days felt so dark for Shivani. She wondered how it must have felt for her children.

“This happens in married life. That doesn’t mean you have to take the kids and come here. After marriage, your home is with your husband.” Shivani recollects her father’s words when she came back to her parent’s home two weeks ago.

His unexpected disappointment shattered Shivani’s hopes of getting any kind of support. Feeling the weight of loneliness devour her, she remembered her mother’s words, “At least let her enter the house. It’s so late in the night. Don’t talk about anything in front of the grandchildren. Come in beta, and bring the kids. Ramesh, you take her suitcase. I will make the food hot.”

Leaving her marital home in the dead of the night was a testament to the level of intolerance she experienced. Taking her children, she left after a brief call with Gaurav. He was working late or so he said but the music in the background played a different story. His words used up the last straw for Shivani when she asked how long he would take to come home, “Why? Are you with someone at this hour that you want to know how long I will take at work?” he passed a snide remark at her.

She remembered her mother’s life from when Shivani was 10 years old. The fighting and screaming between her parents. Shivani and her younger brother would sit in the other room, hoping against hope that their parents would stop fighting. But some nights, they would run out of luck and forcibly intervene to stop the screaming. It was all in the past and the past did not exist until it caught up to Shivani’s married life. Only this time, she was not about to tolerate it for the rest of her life. Unsure of whether her mother made the right decision to stay with her father, she knew she was about to go in a different direction. Of course, back then, times were different, and so were the laws, but even now, people live with the same mindset that divorce should never be an option. She felt lucky that at least her mother supported her.

PART 2

"These are the documents and some emails, WhatsApp messages, and letters. I hope this helps prove his behaviour with me for all these years. Will these be enough?" Shivani handed over a list of documents to her lawyer that proved Gaurav's level of abuse.

Her lawyer, Ragini, looked at the documents, printed and compiled in a folder. Shivani's descending marital life, labelled against each file from year to year.

"These should do for now," Ragini said, "Keep on looking for such documented materials. During your time with Gaurav, did you ever get to record his behaviour on camera?"

"Not really. The fights would usually begin in the night on weekdays. On the weekends, it would be in the afternoon. I never thought it would come to this, so recording a video on him did not occur to me."

Ragini puts the file aside and explains to Shivani the process that will follow from the fees to the court proceedings. It was a battlefield Shivani never dreamt of being a part of but now she didn't have a choice.

"It will come up to Rs 8 Lakhs and more since this is a contested divorce which means it is one-sided. There will be other complexities including the custody of your daughters."

Shivani took a gaping breath at the thought of the expenses while the pressure of the custody battle was no less a burden in itself. "Is this the total cost of your fees alone?"

"No, this fee includes mine plus the court fees including documentation, notary charges, and so on."

"But I can't afford this much. I don't have an income as high as Gaurav's. A lot of it is going to get used up for my daughters now that I will be a single parent."

"There are a few options you can look for such as legal aid if you have faced domestic violence. I can connect with some departments and let you know what happens. Shivani, I know this is going to be a real battle for you but understand that I am here for you and will see what I can do to make sure that you get through this divorce."

"Thank you, Ragini. That means a lot. It's just that I don't want to be a burden to my parents because of all of this. My father is disappointed in me for making this decision. He somehow feels that we can patch things up. If it were not for my mother's support, I don't know what I would have done."

"I understand. If you want, I can talk to your father and explain certain things to him."

"That's very kind of you but I don't think it will help."

"No problem. In that case, I will explain the expenses that will be involved from here on."

Ragini pulls out a list of requirements. It included the lawyer's consultation fees, filing for children's custody, the court fees, the documentation, the notaries, and so on. She was shown areas where Shivani could partake in mutual agreements with Gaurav from child care to alimony.

"Shivani, I won't sugarcoat this for you. Things are going to get expensive even if you get legal aid. However, once this battle is over and you are out of this marriage legally, there will be another battle ongoing."

Shivani sat silent wondering what Ragini meant. What was this second battle that she sputtered out amid the overwhelming fees that already weighed heavy upon Shivani's shoulders?

"I am talking about the battle after this battle. Things may now seem overwhelming but in my professional opinion, it is what also comes after."

"I don't understand what you mean."

"My clients have often felt absolute relief once they got a divorce. Some of them even get alimony which is fine but many of them, and like I said, mostly women do not know how to use the money they get from either their ex-husband's alimony or the divorce settlement. These days, many women are learning how to save their hard-earned money. Judging by your case, I feel you may not be among those women. If you want to continue leading your life independently and providing for your daughters' education and future, I suggest you get advice for it within this week."

"You mean to say… savings from what I earn?"

Ragini pulls out a visiting card from her drawer, "Yes. This is Ms Sadhana Puri. She is a financial consultant, especially for women. She has dealt with many cases where the woman is a single parent. She is also a good friend, which is why you can trust her to give you good advice."

Shivani takes the card and looks at it. Ragini notices a wave of hesitation over Shivani's face.

"Don't worry. Her services are affordable and you can pay her based on your convenience."

On the way back home, Shivani sat in the auto-rickshaw. Her eyes, on the road, her mind on the list Ragini showed her. She knew there was a long road ahead. Wondering where she went wrong, repeating the events of the past over and over in her mind. What usually took thirty minutes to get home was done within five.

She sat on the sofa after reaching home. It was an early Saturday afternoon. "What did she say?" Her father's stern and heavy voice flew directly towards Shivani, bringing her back from the trance of the years gone by.

"Well?" her father waited, "What did your lawyer say?"

Shivani looks at her father sitting at the dining table having his lunch.

"She gave me a list of expenses that I will have to incur for the settlement.

"Hmm..." he continued to chew his food, "how much?"

"...8 Lakhs."

Shivan's mother bringing rotis from the kitchen heard the amount. She stopped in her tracks before she could reach the table. Looking at Shivani, her steps lost their way.

"Give, give..." Her father draws her mother's attention to the rotis. Rushing to the table, she places two more rotis on his plate. He looks at Shivani and then her mother, "Don't be so shocked. You all came into my life to spend my money and dry me up completely. Your daughter has turned us into a laughing stock for everyone to watch and enjoy the show. I thought her marriage would be the end of my responsibilities but she is back to punish me."

Shivani felt the aching pangs of her father's words. She wondered why he felt the way that he did. The career she chose was a field that wouldn't be too heavy on his bank balance. And yet, the taunts followed her endlessly.

Disappointed, she gets up from the sofa.

"What else did she say?" Her father asked, "Any more surprises? Let us know now. Don't spring it on us later."

Shivani does not respond. She takes her purse and walks into her room, closing the door behind her.

Holding the card in her hand, she reads the name – Ms Sadhana Puri, Financial Consultant. If she wanted to gain any kind of freedom from Gaurav and her father's taunts, now would be the best time.

"Hello, Good Afternoon. Puri's Consultancy, how may I help you?"

"Hello, my name is Shivani Thakkar. I would like to book an appointment with Ms Sadhana."

The call ended after ten minutes. She was scheduled to meet her on Monday at 10 am. Shivani released a sigh of relief, settling with the thought that even if the future looked bleak, at least she was taking some action. The receptionist had asked Shivani for the purpose of her visit. Based on that she was told to bring her salary slips and bank account passbook.

An hour later when she noticed her father asleep in his room, taking his afternoon nap, she went to sit with her mother outside in the living room. They both watched a show together, keeping the volume low so it didn't wake up her father. Sayali and Ankita were in Shivani's room doing their homework. It was a strange yet adorable sight to watch them sit in a room that was once Shivani's as a child. Little did she know that the circumstances she would see them in would come to this day.

Shivani's mother could sense that she wanted to talk.

"So, what did you and your lawyer discuss?"

"8 Lakhs+, Ma. That's all I could think of when I was coming back home. She gave me a list. It was a breakdown of where the money would have to be spent. I don't have that kind of money."

"I will talk to your father."

"Baba talks as though it's my fault that Gaurav is a violent man. Ma, you know why I left? One of the reasons was because Gaurav accused me of having an affair which I was not. But that was not the only reason. A week before finally leaving him, he raised his hand on Ankita. She tried to come in the way when he was pushing me towards the wall."

"You didn't tell me this..."

"How do I talk about it, Ma? I was so shocked that he would hurt his own daughter. I spoke about it with Ragini. She said that without proof, there's not much that can be done but regarding the letters, and other messages I have from him, it should give her something for the case. Apart from that, I am not sure."

Shivani's mother sat, dismayed with the thought that her daughter too had to go through the same experiences she had years ago. Unlike Shivani, her mother was unable to find a way out.

"She has asked me to apply for legal aid. Apart from that, she also asked me to talk to a financial consultant. I will be meeting her on Monday in the morning. Will you help make the kids ready for school and then come with me to her office?"

"Yes, of course. I won't let you do all of this by yourself. Don't worry. Now, I will bring our lunch and don't say no to food. You can't think properly on an empty stomach."

PART 3

"Hello, Shivani. Please, come in. Have a seat." The financial consultant smiles and welcomes Shivani and her mother into her cabin

"I hope you don't mind; I brought my mother along."

"No, it's good that you did. Family support is always good. Next time you can bring both your parents." The financial consultant offered a gentle smile. "So, my receptionist may have asked you to bring a few documents. Were you able to get them?"

"Yes, yes." Shivani removes the documents from her purse, "This is my bank account passbook which is where I get my income. And these are my salary slips for the last five months."

"Okay, great. So, is this all? Do you have any Fixed Deposits in your name or any that your father, or maybe, your husband made in your name?"

"Not really. Even if there is, it's all managed by my father. There is a joint account which my father accessed, but he closed the account a year ago. As you know, because of the divorce, my father and I are not on talking terms. So, I have let go of the fact that I could ask him regarding the joint account and my share in it."

"Okay, no problem. We will deal with one issue at a time. Maybe you can ask your father to provide any details."

Shivani hesitates to talk but finally confesses, "My father hasn't been too supportive of this divorce so I can't entirely involve him right now."

"Oh, I understand. It must not be an easy time for any of you right now. Okay, never mind. We will just have to work with what we have." Sadhana takes the salary slips in her hand with a calculator on her side and starts to study them. "Your gross earning is Five Lakhs, Forty Thousand a year."

"Shivani may get alimony from her husband after the divorce is settled." Her mother points out

"Well, let us go with the assumption that we only have Shivani's salary to rely on for now. This way, we can have a more realistic approach towards her savings. It would be good if she gets the alimony but we should be cautious if the court decides otherwise."

"Tell me, Shivani." The consultant continues, "Are you able to save any amount from your salary by the end of every month?"

"Maybe. I have not kept track of how much gets saved every month."

"Okay, not a problem. From now on, you have to keep track of your expenses. You could try maintaining a digital logbook or a manual register and note down all expenses, from your online transactions to cash payments. Otherwise, just look at your passbook every month and calculate accordingly. When we have an average sum in mind, it will give us some clarity."

Shivani takes out her bank account passbook, remembering all that she was told to bring for the first appointment. She hands it over to the consultant.

"Yes, let's go through these statements together. It seems like a significant portion is withdrawn every month."

"Yes, it's a certain amount I withdraw for buying the groceries and clothing, books, etc. for my daughters. Also, just to take their minds off what is happening, sometimes, I take them out for a meal."

"I understand, children have healthy appetites. But perhaps we can find some ways to regulate spending here. Have you considered creating a grocery list and sticking to it? Maybe even planning meals in advance to avoid impulse purchases?"

"That's a good idea. I had not thought about that."

"Wonderful! It can make a big difference. Also, are you open to exploring cost-effective alternatives? Let's say in this case certain items that are on sale rather than buying expensive brand items."

"Yes, I do that usually because the on-sale items are available and I have started comparing prices."

"That's good. See, at first, these types of decisions may not seem like they're making much of a difference but over time, it will all add up and you will be surprised at the amount you have saved. You will also feel relieved because you won't see your money flow out too quickly and unexpectedly but you will see it growing. You will be more aware of your expenses."

"Yes, of course, I am sure that will make a difference for me and the kids."

Shivani and her mother smiled at each other, feeling comfortable talking to Sadhana.

"Now, let's look at these utility bills. Have you considered switching to energy-efficient light bulbs or using appliances during off-peak hours?"

"After the separation, I have been living in my parent's house so my father looks after the light bills. But soon, I may have to look for a separate accommodation because we live in a small apartment. It has already caused a bit of friction with my father."

"Oh, I see. Okay so, if your father is not supportive enough, we have to consider that too. I think this is why you are saying that you have to look into another accommodation."

"Yes, possibly somewhere in the same area as my parents so that I am closer to them."

"Understood. Since you have a job, we can look at options like applying for a home loan. And while you do so since you have mentioned savings. Let's look at how much you save every month on average."

Sadhana browses through the pages of Shivani's savings account passbook. After making some calculations, she offers Shivani the option of opening a recurring deposit account and adding a certain amount to it every month.

"From what I see, you are saving at least 15000 per month after spending on groceries, bills, and items for your children. I recommend you add a minimum of Rs 8000 every month into a recurring deposit account. We can discuss the period you want to choose for it too. Let's say you choose 18 months, and depending on the interest rate your bank offers, you could get close to a minimum of 7% interest. If we consider this then by the end of 18 months your maturity value will come up to approximately," she calculated again, "Rs 1,52,228."

A Recurring Deposit (RD) is a type of savings account offered by banks and financial institutions that encourages disciplined savings.

It works like this:

You commit to depositing a fixed amount every month for a specific tenure. At the end of the tenure, you receive the total amount deposited along with the interest earned.

Some of its key features include:

- **Fixed Tenure:** You choose a tenure for your RD, typically ranging from 6 months to 10 years.
- **Fixed Monthly Deposit:** You commit to depositing a fixed amount every month.
- **Guaranteed Returns:** RDs offer a fixed interest rate, ensuring guaranteed returns on your investment.

"Oh, I can save that much in 18 months?" Shivani asked, surprised at her capabilities of saving as much. "What if I add more?"

"Yes, you can add more but only when you get an increment in your salary. So, let's keep a cushion for now."

"Okay. For now, I could do that. What about the home loan? How do I apply for one?"

"So, there are a few key areas lenders look at while assessing your eligibility for a home loan. First and foremost is your credit score. Obtain a copy of your credit report from your bank and if the score is good then it will reflect your history of responsible borrowing and repayment. It significantly influences the interest rate you will be offered on the loan."

Shivani's mother listens intently as the two women hash out all the details. She looks proudly at Shivani for taking control of her life. She silently hoped and wished that such opportunities and access to information were available to her years ago when Shivani was a child. Maybe things would have been different, just maybe…

"I will be using some new jargon here but don't worry, you will get familiar with the terms over time. That brings me to the next factor to consider, that is, the debt-to-income ratio. This compares your monthly debt obligations like existing loans to net income after expenses."

"My husband, Gaurav, used to look after these things. Besides, I didn't have much in my name so I never handled any of it. I depended on him for most of the expenditure."

"Yes, in our society, we have been conditioned to believe that it is okay to depend entirely on the male counterpart of the house. In your case, your father and then your husband. But when life takes such turns, the dependent such as yourself feels the most alone. So, my job is to make sure that, money-wise, you don't ever have to feel that way. And don't worry, managing your money is not rocket science. Yes, it will take time like ten years minimum and even more but you will see the difference as each year passes."

Shivani nods her head in agreement, hopeful for a future that she never thought she would look forward to…

"Also, since you don't have much in your name as of now, it might work in your favour.

A home loan, also known as a mortgage, is a type of loan that allows you to borrow money to purchase a property. The property itself serves as collateral for the loan. This means that if you fail to repay the loan, the lender can seize and sell your property to recover their funds.

When you would need a home loan:

Typically, you'll need a home loan when you want to purchase a property but don't have the full amount of money upfront.

Some common scenarios where a home loan is necessary:

1. **Buying a First Home:** This is the most common reason for taking out a home loan. It allows you to purchase a property, even if you don't have all the funds saved up.
2. **Purchasing a Second Home:** If you want to buy a second property, such as a vacation home or an investment property, you may need a home loan.
3. **Home Improvement:** You can use a home loan to finance home renovations or additions, such as building a new room or upgrading your kitchen.
4. **Debt Consolidation:** In some cases, you can use a home loan to consolidate high-interest debt, such as credit card debt, into a single, lower-interest loan.

What you need to remember:

- **Interest Rates:** Home loans typically have lower interest rates compared to other types of loans.
- **Loan Tenure:** The longer the loan tenure, the lower your monthly payments will be, but you'll end up paying more interest over time.
- **Down Payment:** You'll usually need to make a down payment to secure a home loan. The larger the down payment, the lower your loan amount and monthly payments will be.
- **Eligibility Criteria:** Lenders have specific eligibility criteria, including income, credit score, and employment history.

Their conversation went on for another hour until Shivani was motivated to start saving from her hard-earned money without having to depend on anyone.

***

It had been a few weeks since Shivani had arranged for the recurring deposit. She made sure to maintain a manual register to track her expenses. She also made sure to teach her daughters the value of money. She would give them a specific amount of pocket money every month and would ask to make sure that they saved a certain sum every month.

Monthly income	in-hand	Rs 45,000 per month
Monthly expenses	• Groceries • Bills (phone & miscellaneous) • Clothing for Shivani and her daughters	Rs 15000 - 22,000 per month (depending on the items bought)
Recurring Deposit		Rs 8000 per month (7% interest)
Balance income at the end of every month		Rs 15,000 - 22,000 per month

There were times when she wondered whether all her efforts and savings were making any difference but with Sadhana's support and her mother's she continued to endeavour.

"But if I have close to Rs 22,000 left at the end of each month then what if I put that into another savings account? Or, should I just collect it and put it aside?" Shivani thought aloud

"Ask Sadhana and see what she has to say." her mother said. "I remember my aunt once speaking to your grandmother. I must have been 15 years old at the time. Those days times were different but even my aunt used to keep aside some money that her husband used to give her for home expenses every month. Over the years, she had so much money kept aside. Today, income tax officers would have raided her house."

"Really? How much did Naani's sister save?"

"In those days, it was close to 2 lakh rupees. To us that was a huge amount. She was a smart woman, my aunt!"

"Well, I am tempted to keep aside that money as cash or let it just stay in my account but I don't want to risk it since we've entered the demonetisation era. I will ask Sadhana when I meet her next."

Meanwhile, Shivani limited outdoor meals and extra expenses. They made sure to eat out only twice in a month. Some of the clothes that Sayali outgrew were given to Ankita, which helped save additional expenses on buying new clothes. Like this, many other steps were taken to save money and only spent during emergencies or necessities including the bills, education and food.

"I have a good balance in my account since I've started more and cut down on expenses. How can I utilise the monthly balance amounts right now?"

"It's a good thing. What I would suggest is not to put that money into any other savings account for now. Instead, let it build up as it will improve your credit score."

A credit score is a numerical representation of your creditworthiness. It's a measure of how likely you are to repay borrowed money on time. Lenders use credit scores to assess the risk associated with lending to you.

When is a Credit Score Used?

Credit scores are used in various financial situations:

1. **Loan Applications:**
    - **Mortgages:** Lenders use credit scores to determine if you qualify for a mortgage and what interest rate you'll be offered.
    - **Auto Loans:** A good credit score can help you get a lower interest rate on a car loan.
    - **Personal Loans:** Your credit score influences your eligibility and interest rate for personal loans.
2. **Credit Card Applications:** A good credit score can help you get approved for credit cards with higher credit limits and lower interest rates.

3. **Rental Applications:** Landlords may use credit scores to assess the financial reliability of potential tenants.
4. **Insurance Premiums:** In some cases, insurance companies may use credit scores to determine insurance rates, particularly for auto and homeowners insurance.
5. **Job Applications:** While less common, some employers may check credit scores, especially for jobs that involve handling money.

PART 4

18 months had passed and Shivani had already earned a substantial amount in her recurring deposit account, a part of which now she is planning to mark as an Emergency Fund . Feeling hopeful about the future of her children, she smiled more often than usual. Her father, although not completely on agreeable terms, decided to help her with the down payment for a one-bedroom apartment in the same locality. He had saved this for her future. Shivani had promised to pay him back.

A door always opens when others get closed. Did you ever encounter some people you are grateful for the way they helped you face critical challenges? Let us share the angels we revere through your thoughts by scanning this QR Code below.

“We’ll see.” Said her father, sitting on the sofa in their living room while reading a newspaper.

She always felt he was too harsh on her. His bitterness was questionable after the ordeal she went through as a child, and then later as a married woman.

"Am I such a disappointment that you would not let it go?"

"Your children are living in a broken marriage because of you. You have shamed us by getting a divorce."

"So, you're saying that I should have tolerated whatever Gaurav was doing to me?"

"Did you see your mother ever leave me? We are still married even today and after all these years, we learnt to live with each other."

"You used to hit mom. She never left because of what society would say. They would blame her for your violence. She depended on you entirely for almost everything. The only thing she could do was cook the food and clean the house. I don't live in that era anymore. If you cannot accept what I am doing, so be it. *You gave Gaurav your approval. Look how that turned out..*" Shivani gets up to leave, "and don't think I won't pay you back for the down payment. I am thankful that you considered paying for me and my children, your grandchildren. I will pay back every penny, that's a promise."

She walks away. He continues looking at the newspaper but barely reading it.

Over the next few months, the custody battle for Sayali and Ankita went smoother on Shivani. The court decided that she would have custody of Ankita and Sayali while Gaurav, their father, would get monthly visits. With legal aid set in place, Shivani was able to get through the divorce settlement, having to worry a little less about paying the legal fees.

While the court did not agree to spouse alimony, Gaurav had to pay a certain sum for child maintenance alimony for the education and future of their daughters. He had to pay 25% of his monthly income for children, which is how Shivani would get Rs 96,000 every month (Rs 48,000 per child).

Salary after increment	Rs 50,000 per month
Balance savings per month from Shivani's income	Rs 20,000 per month (due to inflation and other included expenses)
Child maintenance for Sayali + Ankita	Rs 96,000 (Rs 48,000 + Rs 48,000)
Recurring Deposit earned after 18 months	Rs 1,52,228
Total savings (not counting child maintenance)	=300000+152228 = 452228

She would meet her financial consultant, Sadhana, frequently to talk about her developments. She had received an increment and while it was not much, she was happy that things were moving ahead in her life.

"I am thinking that by next year once my recurring deposit account matures, I will put an increased amount for the next deposit. By then, I may get another increment. I wanted to run my decision by you before going further with it."

Sadhana thought for a while and then asked Shivani, "We both know that these savings are for you and your children. However, by next year, whatever you save along with the added interest, let us take some amount and create two Mutual fund accounts and invest some in gold . One account for Sayali and one for Ankita. In those accounts, you can also put the money that your ex-husband sends as child care."

"Oh, that would be a great idea. That way, I can save for their future education and marriage as well."

"Yes, it will take years, but if you keep letting the money roll in and continue distributing your payments wisely across these accounts, by the end of ten to 20 years, you will have created a substantial amount of savings not only for your daughters but for your retirement as well."

"I never thought I was capable of doing so much, Sadhana. It is all thanks to you and also to Ragini. Had she not referred you to me, I wouldn't know where I would be today."

"I am truly happy to help, Shivani. Many Indian women think that they cannot handle their money and that it is too risky or overwhelming to understand the process. But it's not! If you give it enough time, get the professional help you need, and apply different techniques for saving, you will realise that managing your money is what will make you truly independent. But believe me, all of this starts with the mind. It is important to think independently. If you believe – 'oh, how can I do this or do that?' then you are already giving up. I am proud of you for keeping an open and independent mindset."

"That is true. I didn't give up, probably because I have children and they depend on me. I think if I didn't have children, who knows whether I would have even considered making an appointment with you last year. I would have just continued working and thinking that I could get by without any legal or financial advice."

Several years had passed. Shivani made a wish and blew out all 56 candles after two deep breaths. Her daughters and their life partners stood beside her, clapping and cheering.

"Mumma, I will give you the first bite." Said Ankita

It was indeed a lifelong promise of savings that Shivani had made for herself and to her daughters. Her father and mother, sitting in the back on the sofa, looked at her. This time, her father's expression had mellowed towards her. The road she travelled, the decisions she made, and the hard work she put into creating a new living for her little family. None of it could be denied.

"Of course, Akku. But, let's first give your Naana and Naani some cake. We know how much they love butterscotch."

Shivani had managed to secure more than 100 Lakhs through her savings. She had also managed to equip herself with the knowledge of mutual funds and invested in it while using professional help and advice. While contributing to monthly SIPs through careful planning and with Sadhana's help, Shivani gained higher returns that amounted to over 70 lakhs in ten years.

Mutual Funds

A mutual fund is a professionally managed investment fund that pools money from many investors to purchase securities like stocks, bonds, or other assets. The fund is managed by a fund manager who aims to generate profits for the investors.

Key Points about Mutual Funds:

- **Diversification:** Mutual funds invest in a diverse range of securities, reducing the risk associated with investing in individual stocks or bonds.
- **Professional Management:** Fund managers, experts in the field, handle the investment decisions.
- **Liquidity:** You can easily buy or sell mutual fund units.
- **Variety:** Mutual funds come in various types, such as equity funds, debt funds, and hybrid funds, catering to different risk profiles and investment goals.

Systematic Investment Plan (SIP)

A Systematic Investment Plan (SIP) is a disciplined investment approach where a fixed sum of money is invested in a mutual fund at regular intervals, typically monthly.

Benefits of SIP:

- **Rupee Cost Averaging:** This strategy helps reduce the impact of market volatility. When the market is low, you buy more units, and when it's high, you buy fewer.
- **Power of Compounding:** Over time, the returns on your investments can compound, leading to significant growth.
- **Financial Discipline:** SIPs encourage regular saving and investing habits.
- **Flexibility:** You can start with small amounts and increase your SIP amount as your income grows.

In essence, SIPs are a convenient way to invest in mutual funds, especially for those who want to start with small amounts and benefit from the power of compounding over the long term.

Let's try this mini exercise based on the above knowledge you just earned.

REFLECTION ON INVESTMENT	EXPLANATION	YOUR ANSWERS
Name your specific goal or investment	What is that life goal you want to achieve and how much money do you think you will need to grow to achieve it?	
When do you want to achieve this goal?	Specify a timeline in years based on how much you earn.	
What if your risk comfort level?	On a scale of 1 to 5, 1 is 'very risk-averse' (prefer safety, even if returns are low) 5 is 'comfortable with higher risk for potentially higher returns' (understand market fluctuations are normal) Where do you see yourself right now?	
Which is the most suitable primary investment for your goal?	Based on the three broad types of mutual funds (Equity, Debt, Hybrid), which type do you think might be most suitable for your primary investment goal and your risk comfort level? Explain your reasoning in 1-2 sentences.	
Consider your monthly income and how much can go out for your SIP.	Consider your monthly income and expenses. What is a realistic, sustainable amount you could comfortably commit to a monthly SIP right now without feeling financially strained?	My potential SIP amount: _________ What day of the month would be ideal for this SIP to go out (e.g., just after salary)? _________

Her daughters had allocated their individual savings alongside their mother's savings. Shivani built her and her daughter's assets to a large sum that helped to enhance the health and life insurance.

"Wow, I am already tired climbing this peak for 6 days. This is the first and last time I agree to a trek in the Himalayas." Saakshi, a fellow trekker said

"Oh, you should keep going for such treks. Keeps the mind fresh and the body alive, especially in your 20s." Shivani said to her fellow trekker "That's when you are the fittest to go on such trips."

"Yes, but you are in your 50s, Mrs Hirani. I was impressed when our trekking leader, Ranjeet…" she continued to pant harder as she climbed. "introduced you as the oldest among us."

"In my 50s? I am hardly that old." Shivani laughed. "No matter what your age may be, always say yes to an adventure. Never miss out." Noticing Saaskshi slowing down on the climb, "Come on, pick up your pace. We are almost there. You will love the view. It is worth all the effort you've made climbing up in the past few days."

They reached the top of Mount Meru. Shivani stood on top and breathed in the magnificent view of the volcano and the yonder. While Shivani gazed amid the turbulence of the lava and the chilli peaks beyond, she remembered the years gone by, the challenges she faced, the triumphs she achieved , being a single mother.

A few years after her divorce settlement, Shivani remarried. With a new resolve, she decided never to depend on her spouse completely but to continue building her fortune and that of her daughters and son, Rahul whom she delivered in her second marriage. Even though her second husband was supportive unlike in her first marriage, Shivani had evolved into an independent thinker, realising her potential was ever growing.

"How does it feel, Mrs Hirani?" Saakshi intervened in Shivani's trail of thoughts, "Coming here the second time?"

Shivani continued to look at the view ahead of her, and smiling she said, "Feels like… I still continue to conquer. And call me Shivani. Why this formality? I'm not even that old."

A Quick Summary of Shivani's journey

Initial Financial Situation:

- Single mother with two children
- Limited income and financial resources
- Dependence on father and ex-husband for financial support
- Lack of financial knowledge and planning

Financial Strategies Implemented:

- **Budgeting and Expense Tracking:**
    - Created a detailed budget to monitor income and expenses.
    - Implemented cost-saving measures like meal planning, bulk buying, and using energy-efficient appliances.
- **Savings and Investments:**
    - Established a recurring deposit account for regular savings.
    - Explored options for home loans and credit scores.
    - Invested in mutual funds through Systematic Investment Plans (SIPs).
- **Financial Education:**
    - Sought professional financial advice from a consultant.
    - Continuously learned about personal finance and investment strategies.
- **Family Support and Collaboration:**
    - Leveraged support from her mother and father for emotional and financial assistance.
    - Collaborated with her second husband to build a stronger financial future.

Key Financial Milestones:

- Successfully navigated a divorce and secured custody of her children.
- Established financial independence through consistent savings and investments.
- Built a significant emergency fund and retirement savings.
- Provided financial security for her children's education and future.
- Achieved financial stability and a comfortable lifestyle.

Lessons Learned:

- **Financial Literacy:** Understanding personal finance concepts is crucial for making informed financial decisions.

- **Disciplined Saving:** Regular saving, even small amounts, can lead to significant savings over time.
- **Diversification:** Investing in various assets can help reduce risk and maximise returns.
- **Seeking Professional Advice:** Consulting with financial experts can provide valuable guidance and support.
- **Continuous Learning:** Staying updated on financial trends and strategies is essential.
- **Family Support:** Strong family bonds can provide emotional and financial support.

By taking proactive steps and making informed financial decisions, Shivani was able to overcome challenges, build a secure future for her family, and achieve financial independence

One-Minute Financial Hack!!!

Implement the 24-hour rule - Before any non-essential purchase(not part of your budget) over ₹2000 put in cart and wait 24 hours. Set a phone reminder. You will know whether you really want it or was it an impulse decision.

Book Club Chat

- Do you think there are many women out there like Shivani who have been conditioned to depend on their husband or other male members of their family for finances?
- Could Shivani have made some other investments that would have helped her?
- Do you think she was utilising her money properly when it came to growing it and distributing her savings?

Potential Financial Roadblocks - How to Handle

1. Lack of Financial Literacy/Dependence

- **Roadblock:** Shivani initially lacked financial knowledge and was dependent on her husband for financial management.
- **Resolution: Seek professional guidance and commit to learning.** Shivani actively engaged with her financial consultant, Sadhana, and gradually educated herself on financial concepts like RDs, credit scores, and mutual funds.

2. Family Disapproval and Emotional Burden

- **Roadblock:** Shivani faced significant emotional challenges and disapproval from her father regarding her divorce and financial independence.
- **Resolution: Prioritize your well-being and long-term financial security.** While difficult, Shivani pushed past the negativity, focusing on her children's and her own future. Building financial independence often requires internal resilience and a strong personal conviction.

3. Managing Multiple Financial Goals with Limited Income

- **Roadblock:** Balancing immediate expenses, saving for a home, and planning for children's future education/marriage, all while dealing with fluctuating income.
- **Resolution: Implement a multi-tiered savings and investment strategy.** Shivani diversified her savings by using RDs for short-term goals and then transitioning to **mutual funds** (especially via SIPs) for long-term wealth creation for her daughters' future and her own retirement. She also meticulously tracked expenses and found ways to cut discretionary spending.

Rathandeep's Kaleidoscope

Life's turbulence can feel isolating, especially when financial independence seems out of reach. But as Shivani's incredible journey reveals, **resilience is your greatest asset.** Embrace professional guidance, for it unlocks possibilities you never imagined. Cultivate **disciplined saving** and **strategic investing**, allowing your money to grow quietly, powerfully, for your future and for those you cherish. Remember, **true independence begins with the mind**, knowing you are capable of conquering any peak, financial or otherwise.

Back in the garden

"I think this is your fifth trek but somewhere else, right?" Damini asked.

"Yes, I love going on treks. I was barely allowed to go on school trips. My father would not allow me."

"So, now you are fulfilling all your dreams."

"You can say that. But I was most happy when I realised that I could provide for myself and for my children without depending on anyone."

"I don't think any of us knew that you got married a second time." Meetha said

"Yes, I never planned on it, especially the first one. I had decided not to go through something like that again but then when I met my husband, he was very different from Gaurav. He encouraged me a lot and was always very supportive."

"Well, being a single mother is not easy, and you were able to work and provide for your children. Kudos to you for working so hard and being so endearing." said Sita

"Thank you all for listening to my story. I am grateful for all the people in my life who helped me navigate this journey with a sense of freedom."

While all the ladies sat wondering how Shivani came through in all those challenges, a strong wind blew across the garden. It was time for the next story.

"Damini, it's your turn now. What do you have for us?" asked Shivani

"Yes, finally, I get to talk about my life. My story starts with when I dumped my live-in boyfriend. Things went completely south from there…"

A REJECTED PROPOSAL AND A FUTURE UNKNOWN

PART 1

'Damini, I should not have dreamt of a future with you. I will send a friend to take the rest of my things. Goodbye. -Deepak.'

The folded paper under the clock on the bedside table said it all. He had left her.

She knew a week was probably too long a wait to keep him hanging. Her mind went round and round as she circled back to that candlelit dinner seven days ago. But what could she have said? She wondered. How many times would she have to say it differently every time he had an expectation?

All his things were gone, his clothes, his toothbrush, even the wall unit in the living room that he bought. Walking around her empty apartment felt like an unforeseen and unimaginable event that she never thought would take place.

Looking at their photo frame on a side table, she was taken back to the night he proposed.

"Damini Kiran Shirodkar! Will you marry me and make me the happiest and luckiest man in the world?"

The chatting, whispers, and chewing gave a screeching halt. All eyes turned to Deepak bending down on one knee. The candle's flame on the dinner table flickered with a subtle breeze blowing across the open-air restaurant. Deepak smiled incessantly while hearing a few people cheering from other tables. With the hope of a future together, his eyes sparkled brighter than the open star-crossed sky above them.

Damini sat frozen with a spoon in her left hand and the last piece of dessert in her mouth. For her, the cheers from other tables and the envious smiles were a blurry drizzle. All she remembered hearing were those four haunting words – *Will. You. Marry. Me.???*

The silence between them grew as Damini relentlessly stared at Deepak's wide-eyed spectacles. In about six seconds, he sensed the weight of his future hanging heavily in the suspenseful air of Damini's awaited Yes. Ten long seconds later, what seemed like a good minute passed sluggishly, and the people at other tables started to feel the awkwardness of her silence.

Deepak's smile turned into a frown. He got up slowly, put the ring back into his pocket, and walked out of the restaurant.

On their way back home in the car as Deepak drove strenuously within the speed limit, just a few but deeply heated words struggled to keep their conversation going.

"Two years, Damini."

"I already told you before we started living together that marriage is not my thing. Only after you agreed did I decide to get into this relationship."

"Exactly," Deepak spoke softly but with a firm tone, "We are living together. So, what is the difference? How will anything change if we get married?"

"Marriage changes everything, Deepak. The dynamics don't remain the same. But how could you just spring this on me in front of everyone?"

"I assumed that after two years you would warm up to the idea of marriage. What is so wrong about that?"

"It is wrong to assume that what I said two years ago will change now. I don't want to marry. I am okay with a live-in relationship but not marriage."

Their ride back home was filled with bickering, disagreements, and more silence.

PART 2

"Nothing like a good blend of Irish coffee to drive away the pain." Damini's close colleague, Soumya sat back at the *Coffee & Cocktails Pub*. Taking a sip, she sat back lazily in her chair.

"Right now, this job is keeping me sane." Damini looks closely at her drink, "Nothing else makes sense."

"What do you mean?"

Western pop music of the 90s played in the background as Friday Retro Night.

"When will all of this change? Demands at the office. Demands from Deepak. Demands from parents."

"What problems do you have? You're so lucky. You are not even married or have kids. What are you complaining about?"

"Oh, so just because I am not married, I don't have problems??"

"You've been awfully cranky these days. Don't bite my head off!"

"Deepak left me."

Soumya got up from her sluggish posture and sat up straight.

"What? When? Why?"

“I rejected his proposal to marry me.”

“He proposed? When did this happen? Why didn’t you tell me?”

“I didn’t want to talk about it.”

“How did he propose? Did he take you somewhere nice?”

“On one knee at the Regis Havana Rooftop.”

“Wow. In an open-air restaurant. That’s romantic and expensive. He must have been devastated when you said *no*”

“Well, technically, I didn’t say *yes* either. Everyone was looking at me assuming that I would naturally say yes.”

“Everyone? He had invited others?”

“No, the other customers at the restaurant. I mean, he just popped a proposal in my face. It was the most dreadful moment.”

“I think you need a strong drink.”

“After that, my father has been forwarding all our relatives’ calls to me. I accidentally answered one of their calls.”

“How did they know?”

“They didn’t know but apparently, my father and mother have been getting more calls these days with marriage proposals from my relatives. They all talk as though without marriage, I am doomed. *What will you do? How will you live alone? Who will take care of you? Blah, blah, blah...* One of my aunts even asked me about my yearly salary and started telling me that at this rate, I would end up on the streets?”

“She knows how much you make, right?”

“Do they ever care how much a woman earns? It’s always about how much the husband will earn and provide, put food on the table, and whatnot.”

“Did I ever tell you why most of my relatives including my parents wanted me to get married?” Soumya reveals, “The whole reason boils down to two things – not being alone and money. Money is the priority but everyone calls it security. Having a life partner is good but it's not so in all cases. In your case, I know about your parents and how their relationship is a total disaster. But it may not be the same in your case. I have seen how you and Deepak get along. But anyway, I think if you show them how much you earn every month, they will probably have a different perspective."

"How much I earn won't make a difference, Soumya. For everyone, I am still single at 27 and that is a problem... for them. And if I tell them how much I earn as a Software Engineer, they will first catch their head, saying *Oh, she earns more than the boy! Now, who will marry her?*"

"See, I get it that you don't want to get married. I support your decision but have you thought about your future?"

"Now you don't start."

"No, what I mean is when two people get married, they have a family. They support each other, not only as partners or emotionally but financially as well. But in your case, once your parents are no longer around, who do you have? I think getting married is not the solution for you but you have to have some plan."

"Okay, so, basically, you mean to say what I should do to maintain some kind of security in the future, especially when I get old?"

"Yes, correct. This thought most often strikes people who have a responsibility for others. In my case, my husband and I have a responsibility for our children so we start thinking in that direction. He and I have an LIC policy for our children. We have an emergency fund set up. He and I contribute a fixed amount to that fund every month and then we also contribute to the LIC. We are also planning health insurance for all of us. It's not easy but we are doing all of this slowly. So, what is happening here is, we have each other's support. Life does not get too overwhelming. Whereas for you, there is no one. I mean, one day if Deepak decides to leave you, which technically now he has; what do you have left? Your job and yourself. How are you going to grow your wealth?"

Damini listens to Soumya. She knew her points were valid.

"Why don't you meet Mrs Naik and see what she has to say."

"Mrs Naik? What has she got to do with this? I mean, I know she helped you once with your project but…"

"Damini, she was the one who suggested that I and my husband open an emergency fund account. She helped me in that mobile app project for *JBB Inc.*, I have maintained a certain rapport with her. She has been working in this company since 2008. Before that, she worked at *L&Z Automobiles* as a project head for ten years. Did you know that she has two children who are settled abroad? 25 years ago, her husband passed away in a car accident. It was really sad you know; the other driver actually jumped the signal. After she became a single mother, she had to take care of her children, so that's how she had to plan everything on her own."

"Oh, I didn't know any of these things. How do you know so much?"

"I go around and talk to people in the company. It's a huge company, Damini. If you want to learn more, you should socialise more."

"Why would I want to meet anyone?" Damini recalls the day she became anti-social just to stay away from questions people asked her about marriage and the interrogations that followed.

"Oh, you are hopeless sometimes. Anyway, listen, on Monday, I will take you to Mrs Naik. You should sit with her and understand how you can plan for your future. You are still 27, you have time. Plan and implement now so you don't have to worry years later."

"What? No, no, wait! Where is this conversation going? I was talking about Deepak and my parents, and now you want to take me to Mrs Naik? I think this is all going out of hand."

"Just do this one thing, Damini. I will be there with you. Trust me, you will thank me later. Do you want to keep working till you are 60, 70, or 80? If you don't, then come with me on Monday."

PART 3

"Are you absolutely sure I should meet her? What will she think? We have hardly ever spoken to each other."

> Sometimes, we need a wake up call. It may not be as pleasant as what Damini is experiencing right now. Frankly speaking, has this ever happened with you or was there a time when this realisation just struck you on its own through life's circumstances? Let us know by scanning this QR Code.

"Damini, this is about your life and living in that apartment and what happens next for you. Worrying about what she or anyone will say or judge you is the last thing you should think about right now."

Soumya grabs Damini by the hand and starts walking.

"If you don't talk to her, I will."

"Soumya, don't be crazy. I don't want to talk to anyone right now."

"Just come with me."

Ten minutes later, Damini found herself sitting across Mrs Naik at a conference table on a Monday evening in an empty room. Soumya sat next to her.

"When my husband died, managing my children was not easy. Luckily his parents and mine were still alive." Said Mrs Naik

The walls laid thick against their conversation amid the wooden table and the leather chairs.

"So, I had some relief until I could be completely independent and take care of my children. Even though I was a working mother, it was not like I was getting fair pay. I am talking about the 90s. One of my male colleagues would get twice as high doing the same job that I did. But for women, somehow the pay was lesser. Whenever I would ask for a pay rise, management would say yes but never gave me a fair increase."

"I am sorry I am dumping all of this on you, ma'am. I know this is very unprofessional of me but Soumya suggested that I come to you."

"Oh, it's no bother. You might be surprised to know that so many women in this company are struggling with managing their money even though some of them get a good income. See, we work in a multi-national company but no one is teaching their employees how to create their own savings. Then when some of them don't get an increment, they feel like they will earn less and then they look for another job but what about the savings? They don't know much, especially the women."

"Is it really that important? I mean, there are still many years to think about this, aren't there?"

"Is it? Do you think there are many years? Several years till you grow old, yes. If you grow old without any illnesses, with enough money to travel the world, pay for your parent's hospital bills, God forbid; or enough money to sustain you after retirement and after your parents are no longer around, but not many years till a sudden accident, till sudden illness, till menopause where your body starts reacting differently to the food you eat or the sickness you experience. I can go on… the list of unexpectedness from life is endless, Damini. We always tend to underestimate time. It travels faster than we can realise."

Damini never looked at her life that way, from the lens of a telescope that stared into the future. "So, what should I do, Mrs Naik? My father has maintained a medical insurance plan for me and I am investing in PPF. It's been five years already."

"That's very good! How much are you investing in medical and how much have you earned in PPF?"

"Well, so far, we have invested one lakh a year in medical and one lakh in PPF every year."

Medical insurance, also known as health insurance, is a type of insurance that covers the costs of medical care. This can include doctor visits, hospital stays, surgery, prescription drugs, and other medical services.

It works by having you pay a monthly or annual premium to an insurance company.

In return, the insurance company agrees to pay for some or all of your medical expenses, up to a certain limit.

A few types of medical insurance plans include:

- **Individual health insurance: Family floater health insurance**
- **Critical illness insurance: Group medical insurance**
- **Maternity health insurance: Senior citizen health insurance**

A **Public Provident Fund (PPF)** is a long-term investment scheme offered by the Indian government. It's a popular choice for individuals looking for a safe and tax-efficient way to save for their financial goals, especially retirement.

Why is it needed?

- **Long-term savings:** PPF is an excellent tool for long-term financial planning, such as retirement savings or child's education.
- **Tax savings:** The tax benefits associated with PPF can significantly reduce your overall tax liability.
- **Financial security:** The guaranteed returns and safety of your investment make it a reliable option for financial security.

"Well, at least you are off to a good start. A PPF is something that will mature typically after fifteen years from the date of investment. But if you prefer, you can commit to a duration of up to 50 years. So, how much wealth do you want to accumulate through this fund will depend on the amount you invest every month, quarterly, half-yearly, or yearly."

Public Provident Fund (PPF) — Growth Calculator

Interest rate: 7.1% p.a. | Monthly investment: ₹10,000 | Compounding: Annual

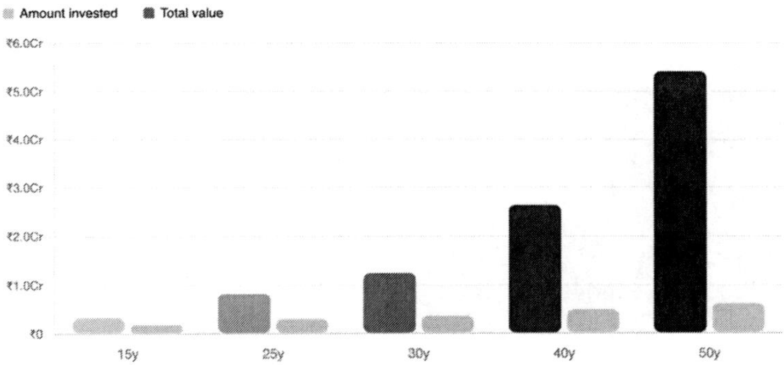

Year-by-year breakdown

Duration	You invest	Total value	Profit earned	Growth
15 years	₹18.0L	₹32.5L	₹14.5L	1.8x
25 years	₹30.0L	₹82.5L	₹52.5L	2.7x
30 years	₹36.0L	₹1.24 Cr	₹87.6L	3.4x
40 years	₹48.0L	₹2.63 Cr	₹2.15 Cr	5.5x
50 years	₹60.0L	₹5.41 Cr	₹4.81 Cr	9.0x

"Yes, that's true. But apart from this, do I need to do more?"

"Yes, for sure. I mean, even if you were married and had kids, I would give the same answer. In your case, you are by yourself and you have made up your mind to live either with someone or not get married, so the alternative to a live-in is living by yourself. It's the same as marriage. If I am not mistaken, since the concept of a live-in is new to me, the alternative to a married life is either living by yourself, getting married again, or going back to live with your family. So, it's only fair that you plan some more savings to keep you secure for your future."

Damini looked intently at Mrs Naik, "So, what else is there to do?"

"Well, you could start with creating an emergency funds account. Create a separate account with your bank where they can automatically deposit a designated sum from your active savings account to another account. It could be a fixed deposit account where you get interest on it based on the period you select. There are many types of savings you can do and this depends on your monthly income. Start with a mutual fund's SIP investment also because the returns are higher based on the amount you invest.

"Is there a certain amount I should add every month to the emergency funds account?"

"Ideally, you can start by making sure the account has a sum equal to three to six months of what you get as income."

"Oh, that's a huge sum."

"It's fine, you don't have to put in all at once. Stagger it across the months."

"Yes, I could do that."

"So, when you go home today, sit and start calculating. Start with adding some columns in a sheet with your yearly income, and how much you need to keep aside for PPF and medical insurance."

A few hours later after dinner at her apartment, Damini sat at the dinner table with a book, a pen, and her laptop. She opened a new Excel sheet and added a few columns. Suddenly, the empty 36 x 48 table settled across her vision and turned into a stark reminder of her time with Deepak. Was it all really over? Will he come back? It was unexpected that he would just leave knowing well about her intentions for the future. What was marriage going to do that a live-in could not provide? She wondered whether she was the one being too rigid or was no one around trying to understand her point of view. While thoughts about her future with him diluted her concentration, she tried to bring herself back to the laptop.

And on she went to type:

Annual pay: Rs 8,00,000 (in hand)

Yearly Medical Insurance: Rs 12,000

Yearly PPF investment: Rs 1,20,000

Balance left from income: Rs 6,40,000

Monthly home expenses

Realising that the amount may be reduced now that Deepak isn't around, Damini decreased the grocery expenses, including removing the cost of Deepak's vitamin tablets and paracetamol for his constant headaches.

- **Groceries:** Rs 15,000 per month, approximately
- **Medical expenses:** Rs 5000 per month (recalling her multivitamins and if she falls sick, she applies an estimate)
- **Shopping:** Rs 10,000 per month
- **Rent:** Rs 75,000 per year (Rs 6250 per month)
- **Utilities:** Rs 3000 per month
- **Extraneous Bills:** Rs 5000 month
- **Money sent to parents:** Rs5,000 per month

After a good half hour of formatting and aligning the numbers, Damini came up with the following data about her expenses:

Yearly / Monthly Expenses - Damini			
Annual pay	**Rs 8,00,000 (in hand)**		
		Per Year	**Per Month**
Yearly Medical Insurance		12000	1000
Yearly PPF		120000	10000
Groceries & house help		120000	10000
Medical expenses		12000	1000

Shopping		60000	5000
Rent		180000	15000
Utilities		18000	1500
Extraneous Bills		30000	2500
Money sent to parents		120000	10000
Balance		**128000**	**12667**

PART 4

They sat across from each other the next evening in the same conference room. It was quiet while the rest of the staff were wrapping up their work. The sun shot shades of gold through the branches of trees aligned in a row. As the golden lines dispersed across the room, Damini noticed how Mrs Naik's wrinkled eyes represented the years of struggle and self-conquering she had to endure.

"So, this is an estimate of what you spend every month and every year. Good, you have shown everything very neatly here." Said Mrs Naik, "By the way, I hope this is not awkward for you?"

Damini looked up at Mrs Naik, "Awkward?"

"Yes. You are sharing detailed expenses with me along with how much you earn. How much you spend on each type of expense."

"Oh, well, I mean… this is a necessary step, ma'am. Also, Soumya kept nagging me about it and whether I started calculating everything as you said. So, I did the best I could. I hope I haven't missed anything."

"Okay, I am happy that you are taking this step in the right spirit. Let's have a look at your sheet." Mrs Naik wore her spectacles and took a closer look at the printed document containing all of Damini's expenses. "So, what is left with you by the end of the year? We can compute an approximate amount based on these details."

Damini focuses on the sheet while Mrs Naik does a basic calculation.

"If you earn 8 Lakhs a year and your expenses amount to Five Lakhs Fifty-Two Thousand a year, then the balance you would ideally save in your account, not counting other emergency expenses or loan payments, etc. should ideally amount to…"

Yearly Income	Rs 800000
Yearly Expenses	Rs 552000
Balance left at the end of the year	**Rs248000**

"I envy that you don't yet have a family to raise or are married. You have all this money to yourself, 1.28 Lakh Rupees per year, give or take. Imagine, how much you can save on this money after 30 years?"

"I can?"

"Absolutely. Now, let's say you invest even Rs 10,000 every month in SIP. Like how you are sipping your coffee one sip at a time . How much would you invest in a year?"

"One Lakh, Twenty Thousand."

"Correct. And let's say you keep investing 1,20,000 every year for the next 10 years. How much would you have saved at a 12-15%% interest rate in mutual funds?" Mrs Naik calculates the amount and shows Damini the calculator on her smartphone.

"Rs 29,64,715? That is 29+ lakhs by the time I am 37 years old." Damini says with her eyes widened

"Yes, now imagine what you could save by the end of 20 to 30 years if you continue to go at this rate?"

"But I do not have any knowledge of SIP or mutual funds."

"That's okay, there are so many ways to learn about it. I can tell you about it too. Financial experts can also suggest the best places to invest your money. All you have to do is start saving for your future, Damini."

Damini smiled at Mrs Naik, hopeful about the years to come.

"So, your next step is to go to your bank where you receive your income and ask them about the schemes and types of accounts they have that are best for you. Then start investing."

"What about the emergency funds account that you mentioned?"

"Ah yes. So, for creating savings for emergency funds, ask your bank about a high-yield savings account or money market account. Opening such an account can help you deposit and withdraw money as and when you need it. It offers a variable interest rate that is dependent on the market conditions and its fluctuations but the funds are readily available."

"What about opening a fixed deposit account? Is that the same as a high-yield savings account? I remember my father would always mention it whenever he came home from the bank." Damini's curiosity started to build up.

"I once asked the same question to my accountant. So, no. There is a difference. A fixed deposit offers a higher interest rate in exchange for your commitment to keep the money locked in for a specific period. On the other hand, money market accounts or high-yield savings accounts or SWipe FD provide you with flexibility to withdraw your money whenever you want, and they also have lower interest rates."

"Then why can't I just create an emergency funds account through a fixed deposit? I will even get a higher interest at the end."

"A valid question but fixed deposits or FDs cannot predict when you will have an emergency. If you do have an emergency, you will have to discontinue or break the FD account which means you will access money before it matures. And because of this, you will face a penalty where the bank will give you back your money but after reducing a certain percentage from your returns."

"Oh, okay. Fair enough. Well, Mrs Naik, I can't wait to start saving. I didn't know that one thing would lead to another. My boyfriend left me and I don't blame him, but soon after that I found myself here with you planning a future where at least I don't have to worry about my expenses or be dependent on anyone by a specific margin. Not that I was with him because I depended on him but yes the expenses were distributed between us and it made things easier. Now that he's gone, I have to plan everything all over again."

"It's not difficult but does require discipline and a cautious approach towards how and where you spend your money while focusing on investments. I am very glad to be of help to you, Damini. You remind me of my daughter. She is a little older than you but she too has the same thought and approach. See, now in some years, you will see the results. Be prepared, there will be some setbacks as we don't know what the future holds but just stay committed to saving your money."

EMERGENCY FUND-RELATED QUESTIONS	**YOUR ANSWERS**
Imagine a sudden, unexpected event that would impact your finances. This could be a job loss, a significant medical emergency, a major home repair, or a sudden car breakdown. Which kind of emergency are you most afraid of?	
Estimate roughly how much money you think that emergency might cost you (e.g., three months of lost income, INR 50,000 for a car repair, INR 1,00,000 for a medical bill not fully covered by insurance).	
Think about the scenario you just described. If you *didn't* have an emergency fund, how would you currently pay for it? (e.g., credit card, personal loan, asking family, selling assets). List at least two ways.	Way 1: Way 2:
Based on what you answered above, how does having an emergency fund change this picture?	

Seven years later, Damini had managed to accumulate more than 19 lakhs in her savings in SIP. In the past five years, she increased the investment amount each year. She even had a very high sum in her PPF account. The high-yield savings account and FD that she had started also gave her gains and all put 50 lakhs together.

Damini sat peacefully in the same apartment where she and Deepak used to live together. She was sipping a cup of tea, looking out the window, watching the cars go by. The phone rings, grabbing her attention back into her living room.

"Hello… hi papa……" Damini's expression changes, "What!!? I will be there." She grabs her purse and heads to the car that she bought two years ago.

She reaches a bustling hospital. Asks the receptionist for the room number and heads over to the elevator. Her foot taps harder on the ground after the elevator crosses each floor. Finally, it opens to the 14th floor. She heads out and sees her father waiting outside the ICU.

"Papa? What happened?"

"She just collapsed an hour ago outside the bathroom. I had to rush her to the hospital. She wasn't waking up. She seemed a bit delirious and then she just stopped responding. They are checking her right now. Let's see if the doctor will come and tell us what happened. I have been waiting here for 15 minutes since they took her in."

A few minutes later, a doctor finally comes out saying that Damini's mother suffered a stroke. "She is in stable condition right now but it was a major stroke. We will have to keep her under observation for some days. You will have to go to the billing counter on the ground floor and give your details plus the deposit money for now."

Damini leaves and immediately goes to the billing counter to pay the deposit. She also filled in the details of her mother's medical insurance. The following days that went by had Damini and her father on their toes, paying for the tests that needed to be done, and the days that she had to take off from work.

A month passed until Damini's mother was finally discharged from the hospital and released to be treated from home. They hired a full-time nurse to make sure that her mother was being taken care of in her father's presence. Damini had to get back to work but made sure she would leave on time every day. She started living with her parents until things got better.

"How much are they charging for the nurse?" asked a relative who came home to visit Damini's mother.

"25000 a month." Said Damini's father

"Oh, 25,000! How much did the hospital bill come up to?"

Damini's father hesitated as he tried to recollect the amount. "It came up to something over 20 lakhs since Shailaja was admitted for a month."

"Oh my God. How did you afford it? Insurance?"

"Insurance did not cover the entire amount but we still had some respite. So, Insurance covered 10 lakhs."

"Oh, so you had to personally spend 10 lakhs?" The relative asked

Damini walked out of the kitchen with a tray filled with three cups of tea. She served the relative and then her father.

"See beta, you get married immediately." The relative looks at Damini while taking the tea cup from the tray, "Now how long will your parents look after you? If something happens to you then they will have to pay for your expenses also. At least your husband will be there."

The father glared at the relative impatiently and took a deep breath as Damini calmly placed the tray on the table and sat beside her father.

The relative continued, "See, your father had to spend so much. It's really too much. You are still here..."

"Damini paid all the bills." Her father interrupted. "She is paying for the full-time nurse as well, and I am very proud of her. She has told me not to worry about the expenses. She will take care of everything."

Damini smiles at her father, savouring the validation at her relative's expense.

"Oh beta, you paid? How come you were able to pay so much?"

"*Funny how 'ending up on the streets' turned into a ₹2 crore portfolio, Aunty.*"

The relative sitting across their sofa experienced a harsh gulp of tea as Damini delivered a subtle yet gently taunt her way. "I have learnt how to manage my money."

"Oh," the relative remembers passing a taunt at Damini over a nosey phone call. "That is very good. Please share your secret."

"Sure Aunty, I will, someday."

A few months had passed and Damini's mother started getting better. She was back on her feet, but was going slow on the house chores. Damini would help in every way she could and so did her father. They had to hire a full time house help.

Even though Damini had to pull out huge chunks of money from her savings for her mother's treatment, she now knew how to recover it. The main aspect she was proud of was that she was able to help get her mother treated when it was most needed. It all together strengthened her resolve to maintain more than one emergency account to make sure that not only her mother but also her father and herself were secure during unforeseen events.

Several years had passed. By the time Damini was 42, she had gained massive wealth. Of course, her journey was filled with emergency expenses from the health of her father to paying for a minor car accident she had. However, as the years passed, she worried less and less about her future which she knew was secure.

Damini looked back at the years gone by as she sipped Irish Coffee with Soumya and her husband. Sunil, her new found love interest, went into their room to fetch a DVD to watch a movie with everyone.

“So, what do you guys think about Sunil?” Damini asked Soumya and her husband

“He’s good. Approachable. Not trying too hard to be validated by us. He’s pretty chill. We’re surprised how you guys met at the hospital during your mother’s physiotherapy sessions.”

“Yes, I didn’t imagine I would meet him there. At the time, his elder brother was admitted to the same hospital. I guess it was fate that brought us together.”

“Well, we think he’s okay,” Soumya said

Damini smiles at Sunil walking out of the room smiling back at her, “I think so too.”

A week later they married and with the blessings of Ma and Paa took the flight to Switzerland. A dream both had cherished together.

Key Financial Steps Taken by Damini:

1. **Budgeting and Expense Tracking:** Damini meticulously tracked her income and expenses, identifying areas for potential savings.
2. **Emergency Fund Creation:** She established an emergency fund to cover unexpected expenses, such as medical bills.
3. **Long-Term Investment:** Damini invested in a Public Provident Fund (PPF) for long-term financial security.
4. **Mutual Fund Investment:** She started investing in mutual funds through Systematic Investment Plans (SIPs) to grow her wealth over time.
5. **Medical Insurance:** She maintained adequate medical insurance coverage to protect herself from significant healthcare costs.
6. **Financial Planning:** Damini sought advice from financial experts to optimise her financial strategy.

7. **Risk Management:** She was prepared for unexpected financial challenges, such as medical emergencies, by having sufficient savings and insurance.

These steps helped Damini achieve financial stability and security, allowing her to navigate life's uncertainties with confidence.

One-Minute Financial Hack!!!

The "Unexpected Shield" Hack: Life is full of surprises, and often, expensive ones. Damini learned this firsthand with her mother's medical emergency. We can be good with our habits and plan a gamification This hack is all about creating a robust **emergency fund** along with habit building

The "Bad Habit Tax"

Every time you do something you're trying to quit, pay yourself:

- Late to work = ₹100 to emergency fund
- Ordered junk food = ₹200 to emergency fund
- Skipped workout = ₹500 to emergency fund

Increase fund size till you get this in order then add a new challenge or habit you want to develop. Keep the ball rolling.

Book Club Chats

- What do you think about Mrs Naik's approach on the way she guided Damini's financial plans?
- Should Damini have invested more in PPF compared to other investment options?
- Are you open to growing your savings through SIPs and Mutual Funds?

Potential Financial Roadblocks - How to Handle

1. Unexpected Major Medical Expenses

- **Roadblock:** Even with insurance, a severe illness (like Damini's mother's stroke costing over ₹20 lakhs) can lead to significant out-of-pocket expenses.

- **Resolution: Combine comprehensive medical insurance with a substantial emergency fund.** Diversify your emergency savings across highly liquid accounts (like high-yield savings) and possibly some fixed deposits that, while incurring a penalty for early withdrawal, offer higher returns for a portion of funds. Regularly review insurance coverage limits and consider critical illness riders.

2. Lack of Financial Independence/Dependence on Others

- **Roadblock:** Damini's initial financial dependency on her father and then Deepak left her vulnerable when circumstances changed.
- **Resolution: Prioritize personal financial literacy and independent saving/investing from day one.** Actively learn about different investment vehicles (PPF, SIPs, mutual funds, bonds , gold , real estate etc), track your own income and expenses, and build your own financial assets. This creates a safety net regardless of relationship status.

3. Dealing with Family/Societal Pressure

- **Roadblock:** Damini faced criticism and unsolicited advice from relatives regarding her personal choices and financial situation, particularly after her separation.
- **Resolution: Build financial confidence and politely assert your independence.** Focus on your well-being and financial goals. As your financial strength grows, external opinions will carry less weight, and you'll have the means to handle challenges without seeking validation.

Rathandeep's Kaleidoscope

- Society mistakes spouses for safety nets. Damini's real safety net? Her emergency fund *and* Mrs. Naik's guidance *and* Soumya's tough love.Ask Yourself: *Who are the people in my life that form my net, ones who will help me enhance my quality of life?*

- *Clarity in intentions is the ultimate act of respect—for yourself and others.*
- *The Freedom to Choose Includes the Freedom to Change" .Damini's "I don't want marriage" stance wasn't rigid—it was authentic. Her later openness to Sunil wasn't a betrayal; it was evolution. Living on your terms means permission to redraw boundaries without guilt.*

Live-in and financial security are separate. A support system is most essential and it can be a group of people and not necessarily a spouse alone. Live life on your terms and respect all around you for what they are in your life for .

Back in the garden

"You are so lucky." said Meetha, "Among all of us, you are the only one who did not marry for a long time ."

"Arrey, why lucky?" Sita asked, "Marriage is not a bad thing."

"No, I mean, it takes a lot of responsibility off your shoulders."

"Well" Damini added, "I had my share of struggles even though I was not married. But one thing I will say is that we can all learn from each other. It's not just that we need to approach a financial consultant. In fact, I learnt a lot from Mrs Naik. Similarly, some of my friends learnt a lot from their relatives like aunts and uncles."

The ladies took a long sigh and saw how the moon shared a gentle breeze with them.

"I am just filled with so much joy. We can take all these stories home with us and share them with other women who may need the same help and guidance as we needed back then." said Geetha, "What do you say, Shivani, Bhavani, and all of you?"

"Yes, of course." Bhavani replied. "If not for these types of evening get-togethers, we wouldn't understand the value of our individual journeys put together. It was a wonderful evening."

"Well, it's time to go home." Shivani wraps her purse across her shoulder. "I am making a promise to myself that after I get home, I am going to plan how to spread our knowledge to other women. They deserve the taste of this freedom that we have all been blessed with."

"Amen to that!" said Damini

The ladies went back home with a smile in each of their hearts. They realised as they left that the stories they shared would forever be unforgettable.

Your Next Chapter - Building Your Financial Legacy

Priya sat at her kitchen table on a quiet Sunday morning, her laptop open, a cup of tea steaming beside her. Exactly one year ago, she had written herself a letter—a promise, really—about the woman she wanted to become financially. Today, she was opening that letter for the first time since sealing it.

"Dear Future Priya," she read, *"I'm writing this feeling overwhelmed and honestly, a little scared about money. I have*

₹8,000 in savings, no investments, and I avoid looking at my credit card statements. I hope by the time you read this, things have changed. I hope you're not still living pay check to pay check, worrying about every expense. I hope you've figured this out."

Priya smiled, remembering that anxious woman from a year ago. Today, she had ₹85,000 in her emergency fund, ₹1.2 lakhs invested across mutual funds, and for the first time in her adult life, she felt genuinely excited about her financial future. More importantly, she had just helped her younger sister set up her first SIP and was planning to start a financial literacy group at her office.

This is the power of taking that first step.

Your Financial Mission Statement

Before you close this book and return to your daily life, take a moment to define what financial success means to you. Not what society tells you it should mean, not what your family expects, not what you see on social media—but what it truly means to you.

Exercise: Write Your Financial Mission Statement

Complete these sentences:

- "Financial freedom to me means..."
- "I want to be able to afford..."
- "The legacy I want to leave is..."
- "Money is a tool that helps me..."

Meera, a 35-year-old graphic designer, wrote: *"Financial freedom means having enough passive income to choose projects I'm passionate about, not just ones that pay the bills. I want to be able to travel with my mother while she's still healthy, support my daughter's education without stress, and eventually start a design school for underprivileged children."*

Your mission statement becomes your North Star. When you're tempted to make an impulsive purchase or skip investing for a month, come back to this statement. Does this decision align with your mission?

The Compound Effect: Your Small Actions, Extraordinary Results

Let me tell you about two friends, Kavya and Reshma, both 25 years old, both earning ₹50,000 per month.

Kavya decides to invest ₹5,000 every month in mutual funds. Reshma thinks she'll start "next year" when she's earning more. Just that one-year delay costs Reshma significantly. If both invest for 30 years at 12% annual returns, Kavya ends up with ₹1.76 crores while Reshma has ₹1.41 crores—a difference of ₹35 lakhs, just from starting one year earlier.

But here's the more powerful part of this story: Kavya's confidence grew with every monthly investment. She started reading about finance, joined an investment club, negotiated better terms at work, and eventually started a side business. Her financial awareness created a cascade of positive changes.

Reshma, meanwhile, spent years feeling guilty about not starting, which created a mental block around money. When she finally began investing, she was still fighting against her own limiting beliefs.

This is the compound effect beyond just money—confidence compounds, knowledge compounds, and small actions create momentum that transforms your entire relationship with wealth.

Building Your Money Mentorship Circle

One of the most powerful steps you can take is to surround yourself with people who support your financial growth. This isn't about finding wealthy friends—it's about finding people who share your commitment to financial wellness.

Action Steps:

1. **Find Your Mentor:** Look for someone 5-10 years ahead of you financially. This could be a senior colleague, a family friend, or someone you connect with through professional networks like LinkedIn or financial forums.

2. **Join Your Tribe:**
    - Look for local investment clubs or financial planning groups
    - Join online communities like Reddit's r/IndiaInvestments or Facebook groups focused on women's finance
    - Attend financial literacy workshops in your city
3. **Become a Mentor:** Start sharing your knowledge with someone just beginning their journey. Teaching others reinforces your own learning and creates accountability.

Sunita, a 42-year-old banker, started a WhatsApp group called "Money Minded Women" with her college friends. They share investment tips, celebrate financial wins, and hold each other accountable. "It's changed everything," she says. "We went from never talking about money to having monthly virtual meetings about our portfolios."

Your Emergency Response Plan

Life will throw curveballs. The question isn't whether you'll face financial challenges—it's whether you'll be prepared for them.

The 24-Hour Emergency Protocol:

If you lose your job tomorrow:

- Day 1: Apply for unemployment benefits (if eligible), update your resume, and activate your professional network
- Week 1: Review and cut non-essential expenses, contact lenders about potential payment deferrals
- Month 1: Consider temporary income sources, adjust your job search strategy

If you face a medical emergency:

- Immediate: Use health insurance pre-authorization for planned procedures
- Short-term: Access your medical emergency fund (separate from regular emergency fund)
- Long-term: Understand your insurance coverage limits and plan accordingly

If you receive a windfall (bonus, inheritance, gift):

- 24 hours: Do nothing. Let the excitement settle
- 1 week: Allocate percentages—emergency fund top-up, debt payment, investments, and yes, some for celebration
- 1 month: Implement the plan systematically

Your 90-Day Action Plan

Days 1-30: Foundation Building

- Set up automatic transfers to your emergency fund (even ₹1,000/month)
- Open a high-yield savings account or liquid mutual fund
- Download and set up expense tracking apps
- Calculate your actual monthly expenses
- Set up one automated investment (SIP) for any amount

Days 31-60: Optimization

- Review and optimize your existing investments
- Increase your emergency fund contribution
- Research and apply for better credit cards if needed
- Review all insurance policies and coverage
- Start your financial education routine (15 minutes daily)

Days 61-90: Acceleration

- Increase your SIP amount or add a new investment
- Set up annual financial review calendar
- Start your money mentorship circle or join existing groups
- Begin planning for major financial goals (house, education, retirement)
- Write your letter to future self

The Ripple Effect: Your Financial Confidence Changes Everything

When you become financially confident, you don't just change your own life—you change the lives of everyone around you.

Your daughter watches you negotiate confidently and learns that women can be powerful with money. Your sister sees you investing and starts her own SIP. Your mother sees you planning for retirement and begins to think about her own financial security.

Anitha, a 38-year-old teacher, says: "When I started investing, my 12-year-old daughter became curious. Now she has her own piggy bank and understands the difference between needs and wants. I'm raising a financially literate daughter, and that feels like the most important thing I've ever done."

Your financial wellness creates ripples that extend far beyond your bank account. You become a role model, a resource, and a source of strength for other women in your life.

Letter to Your Future Self

Now it's your turn. Take out a piece of paper or open a new document on your phone. Write a letter to yourself one year from today. Be honest about where you are now—your fears, your struggles, your hopes. Tell your future self what you commit to doing differently.

Seal it (physically or digitally) and set a reminder to open it exactly one year from now. This simple act creates accountability and gives you a powerful way to measure your progress.

Your Next Chapter Begins Now

As you close this book, remember: every financial expert started as a beginner. Every successful investor made their first ₹100 investment at some point. Every financially confident woman was once exactly where you are now.

The difference between where you are and where you want to be isn't talent, luck, or privilege—it's taking that first step and then the next one.

Your financial journey isn't about perfection. It's about progress. It's not about having all the answers—it's about being willing to learn. It's not about becoming wealthy overnight—it's about building wealth steadily, confidently, and in alignment with your values.

The woman you're becoming—the one who checks her investments regularly, who negotiates confidently, who sleeps well knowing she's prepared for emergencies—she's not some distant future version of you. She's the woman who takes action today.

Your next chapter starts now. What will the first page say?

"The best time to plant a tree was 20 years ago. The second best time is now." - Chinese Proverb

Your financial tree is waiting to be planted. The seeds are in your hands. The soil is ready. Begin.

GLOSSARY

1. Assets

Resources with economic value owned by an individual or entity, such as cash, property, or investments, which can provide future benefits.

2. Budgeting

The process of creating a plan to spend money, ensuring expenses do not exceed income.

3. Compound Interest

Interest calculated on the initial principal and also on the accumulated interest of previous periods, leading to exponential growth.

4. Corpus Fund

A large fund set aside to ensure regular income or to meet long-term financial objectives, often used for charitable or institutional purposes.

5. Credit

An arrangement where a borrower receives goods, services, or money in exchange for a promise to repay the lender at a later date, often with interest.

6. Debt Management

Strategies employed to manage and repay outstanding loans or credit obligations efficiently.

7. Emergency Fund

A savings account reserved for unforeseen expenses such as medical emergencies, job loss, or unexpected repairs.

8. Expenses

The money spent on goods and services, either for daily needs or longer-term obligations.

9. Family Wealth

The cumulative financial assets and resources owned and managed by a family, often spanning multiple generations.

10. Financial Consultant/Advisor

A professional who provides expert advice on managing finances, including investments, savings, retirement, and taxes.

11. Financial Freedom

The ability to manage day-to-day living without financial stress, often through adequate savings, investments, and passive income.

12. Fixed Deposits (FDs)

A financial instrument provided by banks or financial institutions where money is deposited for a fixed tenure at a predetermined interest rate.

13. Inflation

The rate at which the general level of prices for goods and services rises, eroding purchasing power over time.

14. Interest Rates

The percentage charged by lenders on loans or offered by banks on deposits as compensation for borrowing or investing money.

15. Investments

Allocating resources, usually money, with the expectation of generating income or profit in the future.

16. Liabilities

Debts or financial obligations owed by an individual or entity to others, such as loans, mortgages, or unpaid bills.

17. Loan Repayment

The act of paying back borrowed money, typically in instalments, over a period as agreed upon with the lender.

18. Medical Expenses/Insurance

Costs related to health care services, often offset by insurance policies that cover a portion of these expenses.

19. Monthly Expenses Tracking

The process of monitoring and recording daily, weekly, or monthly expenditures to manage finances effectively.

20. Mutual Funds

Investment vehicles that pool money from multiple investors to invest in securities like stocks, bonds, or other assets, managed by professionals.

21. Passive Income

Earnings generated with minimal active effort, such as rental income, dividends, or royalties.

22. Real Estate (Rent-to-Own/Lease-to-Own)

A property arrangement where tenants rent a home with the option to purchase it within a specified period, with part of the rent potentially going toward the purchase.

23. Recurring Deposit

A financial instrument that allows individuals to deposit a fixed amount regularly, earning interest similar to fixed deposits.

24. Rental Income

Money earned by leasing out property to tenants, providing a steady stream of income.

25. Returns

The profit or income generated from investments or assets, expressed as a percentage of the investment's cost.

26. Retirement Planning

The process of determining retirement income goals, and the actions and investments needed to achieve those goals.

27. Saving

Setting aside a portion of income for future use, typically in a bank account or financial instrument.

28. Short-term and Long-term Investments

- **Short-term investments:** Investments expected to be converted into cash within a year, such as Treasury bills or certificates of deposit.
- **Long-term investments:** Investments held for several years, like real estate or equity stocks, aimed at wealth generation over time.